Contents

Chinese food is popular almost everywhere in the world. No wonder! Chinese cuisine offers variety, freshness and lots of flavor. Many Chinese dishes use a little bit of meat to add savor to a large amount of vegetables and rice. That sounds like a recipe for healthier eating, and it is. Stir-frying is a lightning-fast cooking method. Once the ingredients are prepped and the wok or skillet is hot, dinner can be on the table in a matter of minutes. That's another modern advantage to one of the world's oldest and most celebrated cuisines.

Stir-Fry Savvy

Organization is the key to successfully preparing Chinese dishes. There are often many ingredients that need to be cut into bite-size pieces before you start cooking. It's best to have small bowls lined up next to the stove holding the individual ingredients so you won't waste time searching for something at the last minute.

pg. 22

Often recipes call for quickly searing ingredients and then removing them to add back to the pan later. This preserves the flavor of the meat and the fresh taste of vegetables. If the pan is crowded, ingredients will steam and become limp instead of staying crisp.

Why a Wok?

Woks just may be the most versatile cooking vessels ever invented. You can stir-fry, sauté, braise or deep-fry in a wok. They can serve as a skillet, a soup pot or a steamer. Originally all woks had a bowl shape to fit into traditional Chinese wood-

burning stoves. On a regular stove it's easier and better to use a flat-bottomed wok so it is in close contact with the heat source. There are many kinds of woks available, but an inexpensive carbon steel wok, seasoned according to the manufacturer's instructions, works well. Beware of some nonstick-coated models and electric woks. They can't get hot enough to safely handle real stir-frying. You can easily use a large deep skillet instead of a wok. Make sure it will withstand high heat and is is heavy enough to retain it. Rounded sides will make it easier to toss ingredients or remove them as needed.

How to Store Asian Sauces

Always follow manufacturer's suggestions on storing sauces and seasonings. Always keep containers tightly sealed and away from light and heat. Even products that do not need to be refrigerated will retain freshness longer if stored there. Sauces will keep at least 3 months under refrigeration.

Refrigerate:	Store in cupboard:
hoisin sauce	hot chili oil
oyster sauce	rice vinegar
sweet & sour sauce	rice wine
	soy sauce

pg. 20   pg. 60   pg. 42

Glossary

black bean sauce/hot black bean sauce: Bean sauces are made from fermented black soybeans (sometimes called salted or dried black beans). Additional flavorings may include garlic, sugar, rice wine and, in the case of hot black bean sauce, chili peppers.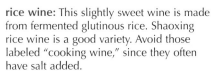

chili garlic sauce or paste: This fiery combination of crushed red chilies and puréed garlic is available in many varieties and brands. The paste is thicker and more concentrated, so if you are substituting, use less.

five spice powder: A mixture of ground cinnamon, cloves, fennel seed, star anise and Szechuan peppercorns, five spice powder is part of many Chinese dishes. It is said to include all five flavors—sweet, sour, salty, bitter and pungent.

hoisin sauce: This thick reddish-brown sauce is sweet, salty and a bit spicy. It contains soybeans, chili peppers and various spices and is used in Peking duck and other classic barbecue dishes.

oyster sauce: A rich-tasting, dark brown sauce made from oysters, soy sauce and, often, MSG. Check the label to see if the sauce you're purchasing contains real oyster extract or just oyster flavoring.

rice vinegar: Both Chinese and Japanese rice vinegars are made from fermented glutinous (sweet) rice. They are milder than regular white vinegars and also have a bit of sweetness.

rice wine: This slightly sweet wine is made from fermented glutinous rice. Shaoxing rice wine is a good variety. Avoid those labeled "cooking wine," since they often have salt added.

shiitake mushrooms: Shiitakes can be purchased fresh or dried. The dried ones are often called Chinese black mushrooms. The meaty texture and flavor of shiitakes works well in many preparations. The stems of shiitakes are woody and tough. Discard them or save them for flavoring soup or stock.

soy sauce: The quality of soy sauce can vary greatly. It is made from soybeans and roasted grain (usually wheat). Light soy sauce is the commonly available variety (not to be confused with lower-sodium or "lite" soy). Dark soy sauce has been aged longer and is thicker and sweeter.

straw mushrooms: Traditionally grown on straw used in rice paddies, straw mushrooms are available in cans in Asian markets. They are sometimes labeled "peeled" or "unpeeled," which refers to whether or not the caps have opened. Rinse carefully and drain straw mushrooms before using them.

tofu: Versatile tofu, also called bean curd, is a custard-like cake pressed from cooked ground soybeans. You can purchase it in soft, firm or extra-firm styles. Bland by itself, tofu readily takes on the flavors of whatever it is cooked with. It is low in calories, high in protein and cholesterol free.

Starters & Sides

Chinese Chicken Salad

4 cups chopped bok choy
3 cups diced cooked chicken
1 cup shredded carrots
2 tablespoons minced chives or green onions
2 tablespoons hot chili sauce with garlic*
1½ tablespoons peanut or canola oil
1 tablespoon balsamic vinegar
1 tablespoon soy sauce
1 teaspoon minced fresh ginger

*Hot chili sauce with garlic is available in the Asian foods section of most supermarkets.

1. Place bok choy, chicken, carrots and chives in serving bowl.

2. Combine chili sauce, oil, vinegar, soy sauce and ginger in small bowl; mix well. Pour over chicken mixture; toss gently.

Makes 4 servings

Hot and Sour Soup

1 package (1 ounce) dried shiitake mushrooms
4 ounces firm tofu, drained
4 cups chicken broth
3 tablespoons white vinegar
2 tablespoons soy sauce
1/2 to 1 teaspoon hot chili oil
1/4 teaspoon white pepper
1 cup shredded cooked pork, chicken or turkey
1/2 cup drained canned bamboo shoots, cut into thin strips
3 tablespoons water
2 tablespoons cornstarch
1 egg white, lightly beaten
1/4 cup thinly sliced green onions or chopped fresh cilantro
1 teaspoon dark sesame oil

1. Place mushrooms in small bowl; cover with warm water. Soak 20 minutes to soften. Drain; squeeze out excess water. Discard stems; slice caps. Press tofu lightly between paper towels; cut into 1/2-inch squares or triangles.

2. Combine broth, vinegar, soy sauce, chili oil and white pepper in medium saucepan. Bring to a boil over high heat. Reduce heat to medium; simmer 2 minutes.

3. Stir in mushrooms, tofu, pork and bamboo shoots; heat through.

4. Blend water into cornstarch until smooth. Stir into soup. Cook and stir 4 minutes or until soup boils and thickens.

5. Remove from heat. Stirring constantly in one direction, slowly pour egg white in thin stream into soup. Stir in green onions and sesame oil. Ladle into soup bowls. *Makes 4 to 6 servings*

Shrimp Toast

12 large raw shrimp, peeled and deveined (with tails on)
1 egg
2 tablespoons plus 1½ teaspoons cornstarch
¼ teaspoon salt
   Dash black pepper
3 slices white sandwich bread, cut into triangles
1 hard-cooked egg yolk, cut into ½-inch pieces
1 slice (1 ounce) cooked ham, cut into ½-inch pieces
1 green onion, finely chopped
   Vegetable oil for frying

1. Cut deep slit down back of each shrimp; press gently with fingers to flatten.

2. Beat egg, cornstarch, salt and pepper in large bowl until blended. Add shrimp; toss to coat well.

3. Drain each shrimp and press, cut side down, into each piece of bread. Brush small amount of leftover egg mixture onto each shrimp.

4. Place one piece each of egg yolk and ham and scant ¼ teaspoon green onion on top of each shrimp.

5. Heat about 1 inch oil in wok or large skillet over medium-high heat to 375°F. Add three or four bread pieces at a time; cook 1 to 2 minutes, then spoon hot oil over the appetizers until shrimp is cooked through and toast is golden brown. Drain on paper towels. *Makes 12 appetizers*

Chinatown Stuffed Mushrooms

24 large mushrooms (about 1 pound)
½ pound ground turkey
1 clove garlic, minced
¼ cup dry bread crumbs
¼ cup thinly sliced green onions
3 tablespoons soy sauce, divided
1 egg white, lightly beaten
1 teaspoon minced fresh ginger
⅛ teaspoon red pepper flakes (optional)

1. Remove stems from mushrooms; finely chop enough stems to equal 1 cup. Cook turkey, chopped stems and garlic in medium skillet over medium-high heat until turkey is no longer pink, stirring to break up meat. Drain fat. Stir in bread crumbs, green onions, 2 tablespoons soy sauce, egg white, ginger and pepper flakes, if desired; mix well.

2. Preheat broiler. Line broiler pan with foil; insert broiler rack. Coat broiler rack with nonstick cooking spray.

3. Brush mushroom caps lightly with remaining 1 tablespoon soy sauce; spoon about 2 teaspoons stuffing into each mushroom cap.* Place stuffed mushrooms on prepared broiler rack. Broil 4 to 5 inches from heat 5 to 6 minutes or until heated through.   *Makes 24 appetizers*

Mushrooms can be made ahead to this point; cover and refrigerate up to 24 hours. Add 1 to 2 minutes to broiling time for chilled mushrooms.

Pot Stickers

  2 cups all-purpose flour
  ³/₄ cup plus 2 tablespoons boiling water
  ¹/₂ cup very finely chopped napa cabbage
  8 ounces lean ground pork
  2 tablespoons finely chopped water chestnuts
  1 green onion, finely chopped
1¹/₂ teaspoons cornstarch
1¹/₂ teaspoons rice wine or dry sherry
1¹/₂ teaspoons soy sauce
  ¹/₂ teaspoon minced fresh ginger
  ¹/₂ teaspoon dark sesame oil
  ¹/₄ teaspoon sugar
  2 tablespoons vegetable oil, divided
  ²/₃ cup chicken broth, divided
    Soy sauce, vinegar and chili oil

1. Place flour in large bowl; make well in center. Pour in boiling water; stir with wooden spoon until dough forms.

2. On lightly floured surface, knead dough until smooth and satiny, about 5 minutes. Cover dough; let rest 30 minutes.

3. For filling, squeeze cabbage to remove as much moisture as possible; place in large bowl. Add pork, water chestnuts, green onion, cornstarch, rice wine, soy sauce, ginger, sesame oil and sugar; mix well.

4. Divide dough into two equal portions; cover one portion with plastic wrap or clean towel while working with other portion. On lightly floured surface, roll out dough to ¹/₈-inch thickness. Cut out 3-inch circles with round cookie cutter or top of clean empty can.

5. Place 1 rounded teaspoon filling in center of each dough circle.

continued on page 14

Pot Stickers, continued

6. To shape each pot sticker, lightly moisten edges of one dough circle with water; fold in half. Starting at one end, pinch edges together, making four pleats along edge; set dumpling down firmly, seam side up. Cover finished dumplings while shaping remaining dumplings. (Cook dumplings immediately, refrigerate for up to 4 hours or freeze in resealable bag.)

7. Heat 1 tablespoon vegetable oil in large nonstick skillet over medium heat. Place half of pot stickers in skillet, seam side up. (If cooking frozen dumplings, do not thaw.) Cook until bottoms are golden brown, 5 to 6 minutes.

8. Pour in ⅓ cup chicken broth; cover tightly. Reduce heat to low. Simmer until all liquid is absorbed, about 10 minutes (15 minutes if frozen). Repeat with remaining vegetable oil, dumplings and chicken broth.

9. Serve with soy sauce, vinegar and chili oil for dipping.

Makes about 3 dozen

You can make homemade pot stickers even if you don't have time to make the dough and roll it out. Just purchase wonton wrappers available in the refrigerated produce section of most markets. This time-saving trick is even used in some restaurant kitchens. Feel free to vary the filling to suit personal tastes as well. Pot stickers are delicious filled with seafood, any kind of ground meat or finely chopped vegetables.

Dry-Cooked Green Beans

4 ounces lean ground pork or turkey
2 tablespoons plus 1 teaspoon soy sauce, divided
2 tablespoons plus 1 teaspoon rice wine or dry sherry, divided
½ teaspoon dark sesame oil
2 tablespoons water
1 teaspoon sugar
3 cups vegetable oil
1 pound fresh green beans, trimmed and cut into 2-inch lengths
1 tablespoon sliced green onion

1. Combine pork, 1 teaspoon soy sauce, 1 teaspoon rice wine and sesame oil in medium bowl; mix well. Set aside.

2. Combine water, sugar, remaining 2 tablespoons soy sauce and remaining 2 tablespoons rice wine in small bowl; mix well. Set aside.

3. Heat vegetable oil in wok over medium-high heat until oil registers 375°F on deep-fry thermometer. Carefully add ½ of beans and fry 2 to 3 minutes or until beans blister and are crisp-tender. Remove beans with slotted spoon to paper towels; drain. When oil returns to 375°F, repeat with remaining beans.

4. Pour off oil; heat wok over medium-high heat 30 seconds. Add pork mixture and stir-fry about 2 minutes or until well browned. Add beans and soy sauce mixture; toss until heated through. Transfer to serving dish. Sprinkle with green onion. *Makes 4 servings*

Ginger Plum Spareribs

1 jar (10 ounces) damson plum preserves or apple jelly
⅓ cup KARO® Light or Dark Corn Syrup
⅓ cup soy sauce
¼ cup chopped green onions
2 cloves garlic, minced
2 teaspoons ground ginger
2 pounds pork spareribs, trimmed, cut into serving pieces

1. In small saucepan combine preserves, corn syrup, soy sauce, green onions, garlic and ginger. Stirring constantly, cook over medium heat until melted and smooth.

2. Pour into 11×7×2-inch baking dish. Add ribs, turning to coat. Cover; refrigerate several hours or overnight, turning once.

3. Remove ribs from marinade; place on rack in shallow baking pan.

4. Bake in 350°F oven about 1 hour or until tender, turning occasionally and basting with marinade. Do not baste during last 5 minutes of cooking.

Makes about 20 appetizer or 4 main-dish servings

Ginger Plum Chicken Wings: Omit spareribs. Follow recipe for Ginger Plum Spareribs. Use 2½ pounds chicken wings, separated at the joints (tips discarded). Bake 45 minutes, basting with marinade. Do not baste during last 5 minutes of cooking.

Prep Time: 15 minutes, plus marinating
Bake Time: 1 hour

Hong Kong Fried Rice Cakes

1 box (about 6 ounces) chicken-flavored rice mix
1/2 cup sliced green onions
2 eggs, beaten
2 tablespoons chopped fresh parsley
1 tablespoon hoisin sauce
1 tablespoon soy sauce
1 teaspoon minced fresh ginger
1 clove garlic, minced
2 to 3 tablespoons vegetable oil

1. Prepare rice according to package directions, omitting butter. Cover and refrigerate one hour or until completely chilled. Add remaining ingredients, except oil, to rice; mix well. Form rice mixture into cakes, 3 inches in diameter.

2. Heat 1 tablespoon oil in large skillet over medium heat. Cook cakes in batches 3 to 4 minutes on each side or until golden brown. Add additional oil to skillet as needed. *Makes 4 to 6 servings*

tip

Hoisin sauce is made of soybeans, garlic, chili peppers and spices. The flavor is a distinctive blend of salty, spicy and sweet. Hoisin sauce is easy to find in the Asian aisle of most supermarkets in either bottles or cans. After opening, refrigerate bottled hoisin sauces. Canned hoisin should be transferred to a non-metallic container before refrigerating.

Wonton Soup

4 ounces ground pork, chicken or turkey

¼ cup finely chopped water chestnuts

2 tablespoons soy sauce, divided

1 egg white, lightly beaten

1 teaspoon minced fresh ginger

12 wonton wrappers

1 can (46 ounces) chicken broth

1½ cups sliced spinach

1 cup thinly sliced cooked pork (optional)

½ cup diagonally sliced green onions

1 tablespoon dark sesame oil

Shredded carrot (optional)

1. Combine ground pork, water chestnuts, 1 tablespoon soy sauce, egg white and ginger in small bowl; mix well.

2. Place 1 wonton wrapper with point toward edge of counter. Mound 1 teaspoon filling near bottom point. Fold bottom point over filling, then roll wrapper over once. Moisten inside points with water. Bring side points together below the filling, overlapping slightly; press together firmly to seal. Repeat with remaining wrappers and filling.* Keep finished wontons covered with plastic wrap, while filling remaining wrappers.

3. Combine broth and remaining 1 tablespoon soy sauce in large saucepan. Bring to a boil over high heat. Reduce heat to medium; add wontons. Simmer, uncovered, 4 minutes, or until filling is cooked through.

4. Stir in spinach, cooked pork, if desired, and green onions; remove from heat. Stir in sesame oil. Ladle into soup bowls. Garnish with shredded carrot.

Makes 2 servings

*Wontons may be made ahead to this point; cover and refrigerate up to 8 hours or freeze up to 3 months. Proceed as above, if using refrigerated wontons. Increase simmer time to 6 minutes, if using frozen wontons.

Menu Classics

Chinese Sweet and Sour Vegetables

3 cups broccoli florets
2 medium carrots, diagonally sliced
1 large red bell pepper, cut into short, thin strips
$^{1}/_{4}$ cup water
2 teaspoons cornstarch
1 teaspoon sugar
$^{1}/_{3}$ cup unsweetened pineapple juice
1 tablespoon rice vinegar
1 tablespoon soy sauce
$^{1}/_{2}$ teaspoon dark sesame oil
$^{1}/_{4}$ cup chopped fresh cilantro (optional)

1. Combine broccoli, carrots and bell pepper in large skillet with tight-fitting lid. Add water; bring to a boil over high heat. Reduce heat to medium. Cover and steam 4 minutes or until vegetables are crisp-tender.

2. Meanwhile, combine cornstarch and sugar in small bowl. Blend in pineapple juice, vinegar and soy sauce until smooth.

3. Drain vegetables. Stir pineapple mixture and add to skillet. Cook and stir 2 minutes or until sauce boils and thickens.

4. Return vegetables to skillet; toss with sauce. Stir in sesame oil. Garnish with cilantro.   *Makes 4 servings*

Cashew Beef

2 tablespoons cooking oil

8 ounces beef (flank steak, skirt steak, top sirloin or fillet mignon), cut into strips ¼ inch thick

3 tablespoons LEE KUM KEE® Premium Brand, Panda Brand or Choy Sun Oyster Sauce

¼ cup *each* red and green bell pepper, cut into 1-inch strips

2 stalks celery, cut into ½-inch slices

½ cup carrots, cut into ½-inch slices

¼ cup small button mushrooms, cut into halves

2 tablespoons LEE KUM KEE® Soy Sauce

1 green onion, chopped

2 tablespoons cashews, toasted*

1 tablespoon LEE KUM KEE® Chili Garlic Sauce or Sriracha Chili Sauce

Cashews can be toasted in wok or skillet prior to cooking.

1. Heat wok or skillet over high heat until hot. Add oil, beef and LEE KUM KEE Oyster Sauce; cook until beef is half done.

2. Add bell peppers, celery, carrots, mushrooms and LEE KUM KEE Soy Sauce; stir-fry until vegetables are crisp-tender. Stir in green onion and cashews. Add Chili Garlic Sauce or Sriracha Chili Sauce for spiciness or use as dipping sauce.

Makes 2 servings

Moo Goo Gai Pan

1 package (1 ounce) dried shiitake mushrooms
¼ cup soy sauce
2 tablespoons rice vinegar
3 cloves garlic, minced
1 pound boneless skinless chicken breasts
½ cup chicken broth
1 tablespoon cornstarch
2 tablespoons peanut or vegetable oil, divided
1 can (about 7 ounces) straw mushrooms, rinsed and drained
3 green onions, cut into 1-inch pieces
    Hot cooked Chinese egg noodles or rice

1. Place dried mushrooms in small bowl; cover with warm water. Soak 20 minutes to soften. Drain; squeeze out excess water. Discard stems; slice caps.

2. Combine soy sauce, vinegar and garlic in medium bowl. Cut chicken crosswise into ½-inch strips. Toss chicken with soy sauce mixture. Marinate at room temperature 20 minutes. Blend broth into cornstarch in small bowl until smooth.

3. Heat 1 tablespoon oil in wok or large skillet over medium-high heat. Drain chicken; reserve marinade. Add chicken to wok; stir-fry chicken 3 minutes or until cooked through. Remove and reserve.

4. Heat remaining 1 tablespoon oil in wok; add dried and straw mushrooms and green onions. Stir-fry 1 minute.

5. Stir broth mixture and add to wok along with reserved marinade. Stir-fry 1 minute or until sauce boils and thickens. Return chicken along with any accumulated juices to wok; heat through. Serve over noodles or rice.

Makes 4 servings

Orange Beef

1 pound boneless beef top sirloin or tenderloin steaks
2 cloves garlic, minced
1 teaspoon grated orange peel
2 tablespoons orange juice
2 tablespoons soy sauce
1 tablespoon rice wine or dry sherry
1 tablespoon cornstarch
1 tablespoon peanut or vegetable oil
2 cups hot cooked rice
   Orange peel strips or orange slices (optional)

1. Cut beef in half lengthwise, then crosswise into thin slices. Toss with garlic and orange peel in medium bowl.

2. Blend orange juice, soy sauce and rice wine into cornstarch in small bowl until smooth.

3. Heat oil in wok or large skillet over medium-high heat. Add half of beef mixture; stir-fry 2 to 3 minutes or until beef is barely pink in center. Remove to large bowl. Repeat with remaining beef. Stir orange juice mixture and add to wok. Stir-fry 30 seconds or until sauce boils and thickens. Serve over rice; garnish with orange peel strips.   *Makes 4 servings*

A spicy version of Orange Beef is a classic recipe from the Hunan region of China. If you wish to add a bit of zip to your Orange Beef, try sprinkling on some red pepper flakes. Chopped green onions or sliced celery would also be authentic additions.

Braised Lion's Head

MEATBALLS

1 pound lean ground pork

4 ounces raw shrimp, peeled and finely chopped

¼ cup sliced water chestnuts, finely chopped

1 egg, lightly beaten

1 green onion, finely chopped

1 tablespoon cornstarch

1 tablespoon rice wine or dry sherry

1 tablespoon soy sauce

1 teaspoon minced fresh ginger

½ teaspoon *each* salt and sugar

2 tablespoons vegetable oil

SAUCE

1½ cups chicken broth

2 tablespoons soy sauce

½ teaspoon sugar

1 head napa cabbage (1½ to 2 pounds), cored and cut into large pieces

3 tablespoons cold water

2 tablespoons cornstarch

1 teaspoon sesame oil

1. Combine all meatball ingredients except vegetable oil in large bowl; mix well. Shape mixture into eight balls. Heat vegetable oil in wok or large skillet over medium-high heat. Add meatballs; cook 6 to 8 minutes until browned, stirring occasionally.

2. Transfer meatballs to large saucepan; add chicken broth, 2 tablespoons soy sauce and ½ teaspoon sugar. Bring to a boil. Reduce heat to low; cover. Simmer 30 minutes. Place cabbage over meatballs; cover. Simmer 10 minutes.

3. Transfer cabbage and meatballs to serving platter. Blend water into 2 tablespoons cornstarch. Add to pan juices; cook and stir until thickened. Stir in sesame oil. Serve over meatballs and cabbage.

Makes 4 to 6 servings

Braised Lion's Head

Barbecued Pork

¼ cup soy sauce
2 tablespoons dry red wine
1 tablespoon brown sugar
1 tablespoon honey
2 teaspoons red food coloring (optional)
1 green onion, sliced
1 clove garlic, minced
½ teaspoon ground cinnamon
2 whole pork tenderloins (about 12 ounces each), trimmed
Hot cooked rice

1. Combine soy sauce, wine, sugar, honey, food coloring, if desired, green onion, garlic and cinnamon in large bowl. Add pork; turn to coat completely. Cover and refrigerate 1 hour or overnight, turning pork occasionally.

2. Preheat oven to 350°F. Drain meat, reserving marinade. Place pork on wire rack over baking pan. Bake 30 to 45 minutes or until thermometer inserted into center of pork registers 160°F, turning and basting frequently with reserved marinade during first 20 minutes of cooking.

3. Remove pork from oven; let rest 5 minutes. Cut into diagonal slices. Serve with rice.   *Makes about 8 appetizer servings*

Kung Pao Chicken

3½ teaspoons cornstarch, divided

5 teaspoons rice wine or dry sherry, divided

5 teaspoons soy sauce, divided

¼ teaspoon salt

3 boneless skinless chicken breasts (about 1 pound), cut into bite-size pieces

2 tablespoons chicken broth or water

1 tablespoon red wine vinegar

1½ teaspoons sugar

3 tablespoons vegetable oil, divided

⅓ cup salted peanuts

6 to 8 small dried red chiles

1½ teaspoons minced fresh ginger

2 green onions, cut into 1½-inch pieces

1. For marinade, combine 2 teaspoons cornstarch, 2 teaspoons rice wine, 2 teaspoons soy sauce and salt in large bowl; mix well. Add chicken; stir to coat well. Let stand 30 minutes.

2. Blend remaining 3 teaspoons rice wine, 3 teaspoons soy sauce, chicken broth, vinegar and sugar into remaining 1½ teaspoons cornstarch in small bowl; set aside.

3. Heat 1 tablespoon oil in wok or large skillet over medium heat. Add peanuts; cook and stir until lightly toasted. Remove and set aside.

4. Heat remaining 2 tablespoons oil in wok over medium heat. Add chiles; stir-fry until chiles just begin to char, about 1 minute.

5. Increase heat to high. Add chicken mixture; stir-fry 2 minutes. Add ginger; stir-fry until chicken is cooked though, about 1 minute.

6. Add peanuts and green onions. Stir cornstarch mixture; add to wok. Cook and stir until sauce boils and thickens.   *Makes 3 servings*

Spicy Hunan Ribs

1⅓ cups hoisin sauce or *Cattlemen's®* Golden Honey Barbecue Sauce

⅔ cup *Frank's® RedHot®* XTRA Hot Cayenne Pepper Sauce or *Frank's® RedHot®* Cayenne Pepper Sauce

¼ cup soy sauce

2 tablespoons brown sugar

2 tablespoons dark sesame oil

2 tablespoons grated peeled ginger root

4 cloves garlic, crushed through a press

2 full racks pork spareribs, trimmed (about 6 pounds)

1. Combine hoisin sauce, XTRA Hot Sauce, soy sauce, brown sugar, sesame oil, ginger and garlic; mix well.

2. Place ribs into large resealable plastic food storage bags. Pour 1½ cups sauce mixture over ribs. Seal bags and marinate in refrigerator 1 to 3 hours or overnight.

3. Prepare grill for indirect cooking over medium-low heat (250°F). Place ribs on rib rack or in foil pan; discard marinade. Cook on covered grill 2½ to 3 hours until very tender. Baste with remaining sauce during last 15 minutes of cooking. If desired, grill ribs over direct heat at end of cooking to char slightly.

Makes 4 to 6 servings

Tip: Use Kansas City or St. Louis-style ribs for this recipe.

Prep Time: 5 minutes
Marinate Time: 1 hour
Cook Time: 3 hours

Cashew Chicken

1 pound boneless skinless chicken breasts or thighs
2 teaspoons minced fresh ginger
1 tablespoon peanut or vegetable oil
1 medium red bell pepper, cut into short, thin strips
⅓ cup teriyaki sauce
⅓ cup roasted or dry roasted cashews
   Hot cooked rice
   Coarsely chopped fresh cilantro (optional)

1. Cut chicken into ½-inch slices; cut each slice into 1½-inch strips. Toss chicken with ginger in small bowl.

2. Heat oil in wok or large skillet over medium-high heat. Add chicken mixture; stir-fry 2 minutes. Add bell pepper; stir-fry 4 minutes or until chicken is cooked through.

3. Add teriyaki sauce; stir-fry 1 minute or until sauce is hot. Stir in cashews. Serve over rice. Garnish with cilantro. *Makes 4 servings*

Did you ever wonder why cashews are always sold without their shells? The reason is that there is a highly toxic liquid within the shell that must be removed during processing. Cashews have a sweet, buttery flavor because of their high concentration of fat. For this reason, they should be stored refrigerated or frozen to prevent rancidity.

Chicken with Lychees

¼ cup plus 1 teaspoon cornstarch, divided
3 boneless skinless chicken breasts (about 1 pound), cut into bite-size pieces
½ cup water, divided
½ cup tomato sauce
1 teaspoon sugar
1 teaspoon instant chicken bouillon granules
3 tablespoons vegetable oil
6 green onions, cut into 1-inch pieces
1 red bell pepper, cut into 1-inch pieces
1 can (11 ounces) whole peeled lychees, drained
Cooked cellophane noodles (bean threads)

1. Place ¼ cup cornstarch in large resealable food storage bag; add chicken. Seal bag; shake until chicken is well coated.

2. Combine remaining 1 teaspoon cornstarch and ¼ cup water in small cup; mix well. Combine remaining ¼ cup water, tomato sauce, sugar and bouillon granules in small bowl; mix well.

3. Heat oil in wok or large skillet over high heat. Add chicken; stir-fry until lightly browned, 5 to 8 minutes. Add onions and bell pepper; stir-fry 1 minute.

4. Pour tomato sauce mixture over chicken mixture. Stir in lychees. Reduce heat to low; cover. Simmer until chicken is tender and cooked through, about 5 minutes.

5. Stir cornstarch mixture; add to wok. Cook and stir until sauce boils and thickens. Serve over hot cellophane noodles.   Makes 4 servings

Beef with Leeks and Tofu

8 ounces boneless beef top sirloin, top loin (strip) or tenderloin steaks
2 cloves garlic, minced
8 ounces firm tofu, drained*
¾ cup chicken broth
¼ cup soy sauce
1 tablespoon rice wine or dry sherry
1 tablespoon cornstarch
4 teaspoons peanut or vegetable oil, divided
1 large *or* 2 medium leeks, sliced (white and light green portion)
1 large red bell pepper, cut into short, thin strips
1 tablespoon dark sesame oil (optional)
   Hot cooked noodles (optional)

*To firm tofu for stir-frying, slice tofu block horizontally into 2 pieces. Place on cutting board between layers of paper towels. Put another board or plate on top; add a weight to press moisture out of tofu. Let stand about 15 minutes.

1. Cut beef lengthwise in half, then crosswise into ⅛-inch slices. Toss beef with garlic in medium bowl. Cut tofu into ¾-inch triangles or squares.

2. Blend broth, soy sauce and rice wine into cornstarch in small bowl until smooth.

3. Heat 2 teaspoons peanut oil in large, deep skillet over medium-high heat. Add half of beef mixture; stir-fry 2 minutes or until beef is barely pink in center. Remove to large bowl. Repeat with remaining beef. Remove and set aside.

4. Add remaining 2 teaspoons peanut oil to skillet. Add leek and bell pepper; stir-fry 3 minutes or until bell pepper is crisp-tender. Stir broth mixture; add to skillet with tofu. Stir-fry 2 minutes or until sauce boils and thickens and tofu is hot, stirring frequently.

5. Return beef along with any accumulated juices to skillet; heat through. Stir in sesame oil, if desired. Serve over noodles, if desired.

Makes 4 servings

Sizzling Stir-Fries

Chinese Pork & Vegetable Stir-Fry

2 tablespoons BERTOLLI® Olive Oil, divided
1 pound pork tenderloin or boneless beef sirloin, cut into
   ¼-inch slices
6 cups assorted fresh vegetables*
1 can (8 ounces) sliced water chestnuts, drained
1 envelope LIPTON® RECIPE SECRETS® Onion Soup Mix
¾ cup water
½ cup orange juice
1 tablespoon soy sauce
¼ teaspoon garlic powder

Use any combination of the following: broccoli florets; thinly sliced red or green bell peppers; snow peas or thinly sliced carrots.

1. In 12-inch skillet, heat 1 tablespoon olive oil over medium-high heat; brown pork. Remove and set aside.

2. In same skillet, heat remaining 1 tablespoon olive oil and cook assorted fresh vegetables, stirring occasionally, 5 minutes. Stir in water chestnuts, soup mix blended with water, orange juice, soy sauce and garlic powder. Bring to a boil over high heat. Reduce heat to low and simmer, uncovered, 3 minutes. Return pork to skillet and cook 1 minute or until heated through.

Makes about 4 servings

Three-Pepper Steak

1 boneless beef top sirloin or beef flank steak (about 1 pound)
3 tablespoons soy sauce
1 tablespoon cornstarch
1 tablespoon brown sugar
1½ teaspoons dark sesame oil
¼ teaspoon red pepper flakes
3 tablespoons vegetable oil, divided
1 small green bell pepper, cut into ½-inch strips
1 small red bell pepper, cut into ½-inch strips
1 small yellow bell pepper, cut into ½-inch strips
1 medium onion, cut into 1-inch pieces
2 cloves garlic, finely chopped
Hot cooked rice

1. Cut beef in half lengthwise, then crosswise into ¼-inch-thick slices. Combine soy sauce, cornstarch, brown sugar, sesame oil and red pepper flakes in medium bowl; stir until smooth. Add beef and toss to coat; set aside.

2. Heat 1 tablespoon vegetable oil in wok over high heat. Add bell pepper strips; stir-fry until crisp-tender. Remove to large bowl. Add 1 tablespoon vegetable oil and heat 30 seconds. Add half of beef mixture to wok; stir-fry until well browned. Remove beef to bowl with bell peppers. Repeat with remaining 1 tablespoon vegetable oil and beef mixture.

3. Reduce heat to medium. Add onion; stir-fry about 3 minutes or until softened. Add garlic; stir-fry 30 seconds. Return bell peppers, beef and any accumulated juices to wok; cook until heated through. Spoon rice into serving dish; top with beef and vegetable mixture. *Makes 4 servings*

Seafood & Vegetable Stir-Fry

2 teaspoons olive oil
½ medium red or yellow bell pepper, cut into strips
½ medium onion, cut into wedges
10 snow peas, cut diagonally in half
1 clove garlic, minced
6 ounces medium cooked shrimp
2 tablespoons stir-fry sauce
1 cup hot cooked rice

1. Heat oil in large nonstick skillet over medium-high heat. Add bell pepper, onion and snow peas; stir-fry 4 minutes. Add garlic; stir-fry 1 minute or until vegetables are crisp-tender.

2. Add shrimp and stir-fry sauce; stir-fry 1 to 2 minutes or until hot. Serve over rice. *Makes 2 servings*

Shrimp can be purchased in many different sizes, cooked or uncooked and with or without their shells. Most supermarket shrimp is sold frozen or has been thawed for convenience. There are about 31 to 35 medium shrimp per pound. Because it is extremely perishable, cooked shrimp should be stored in the coldest part of your refrigerator and consumed within a day or two.

Stir-Fried Eggplant and Tofu

1 green onion
4 ounces lean ground pork
2 cloves garlic, minced
1 teaspoon minced fresh ginger
$\frac{1}{2}$ teaspoon dark sesame oil
4 ounces firm tofu
$\frac{1}{2}$ cup chicken broth
$\frac{1}{2}$ teaspoon cornstarch
1 pound Asian eggplants
2 tablespoons peanut oil
1 tablespoon soy sauce
1 teaspoon chili garlic sauce
$\frac{1}{2}$ teaspoon sugar

1. Mince white part of green onion. Cut green part of onion diagonally into 1$\frac{1}{2}$-inch lengths; reserve for garnish.

2. Combine pork, minced green onion, garlic, ginger and sesame oil in small bowl.

3. Drain tofu on paper towels. Cut into $\frac{1}{2}$-inch cubes.

4. Stir chicken broth into cornstarch in small bowl; set aside.

5. To prepare eggplants, trim off cap and stem ends; cut lengthwise into quarters, then into 1-inch pieces.

6. Heat peanut oil in wok or large skillet over high heat. Add eggplant; stir-fry 5 to 6 minutes or until tender. Add tofu; stir-fry 1 minute. Remove eggplant and tofu from wok; set aside.

7. Add pork mixture to wok; stir fry 2 minutes or until browned. Add soy sauce, chili garlic sauce and sugar; cook and stir until heated through.

8. Return eggplant and tofu to wok. Stir cornstarch mixture; add to wok. Cook and stir until sauce thickens.   Makes 4 servings

Stir-Fried Eggplant and Tofu

Szechuan Vegetable Stir-Fry

8 ounces firm tofu, drained
1 cup vegetable broth, divided
½ cup orange juice
⅓ cup soy sauce
1 to 2 teaspoons hot chili oil
½ teaspoon whole fennel seeds
½ teaspoon black pepper
2 tablespoons cornstarch
3 tablespoons vegetable oil
1 cup sliced green onions
3 medium carrots, sliced
3 cloves garlic, minced
2 teaspoons minced fresh ginger
¼ pound mushrooms, sliced
1 medium red bell pepper, cut into 1-inch squares
¼ pound snow peas, cut diagonally in half
8 ounces broccoli florets, steamed
½ cup peanuts
4 to 6 cups hot cooked rice

1. Slice tofu block horizontally into 2 pieces. Place on cutting board between layers of paper towels. Put another board or plate on top; add a weight to press moisture out of tofu. Let stand about 15 minutes.

2. Cut tofu into cubes; place in baking dish. Combine ½ cup broth, orange juice, soy sauce, chili oil, fennel seeds and black pepper in small bowl; pour over tofu. Let stand 15 to 60 minutes. Drain, reserving marinade.

3. Stir remaining ½ cup broth into cornstarch in medium bowl. Add reserved marinade; set aside.

4. Heat vegetable oil in wok or large skillet over high heat. Add green onions, carrots, garlic and ginger; stir-fry 3 minutes. Add tofu, mushrooms, bell pepper and snow peas; stir-fry 2 to 3 minutes or until vegetables are crisp-tender. Add broccoli; stir-fry 1 minute or until heated through.

5. Stir cornstarch mixture. Add to wok; cook 1 to 2 minutes or until bubbly. Stir in peanuts. Serve over rice. *Makes 4 to 6 servings*

Shrimp with Snow Peas

 1 pound raw Florida shrimp
 ½ cup chicken broth
 ¼ cup soy sauce
 3 tablespoons dry sherry or white wine
 2 tablespoons cornstarch
 2 teaspoons minced fresh ginger
 ¼ cup vegetable oil
 1 (6-ounce) package frozen snow peas, thawed and patted dry, or
    ½ pound fresh snow peas
 3 green onions, cut into 1-inch pieces
 ½ can (8 ounces) sliced water chestnuts
    Hot cooked rice

Peel shrimp and, if large, cut into halves lengthwise. Combine chicken broth, soy sauce, sherry, cornstarch and ginger in small bowl; set aside. In wok or large skillet, heat oil until hot. Add shrimp. Cook, stirring rapidly, 3 to 4 minutes or until pink; remove. Add snow peas; stir-fry 3 to 4 minutes or until soft. Remove from wok; set aside. Repeat procedure with onions and water chestnuts. Add shrimp, snow peas, onions and water chestnuts to wok. Add chicken broth mixture and cook until sauce thickens slightly, about 2 to 3 minutes. Serve over rice. *Makes 4 servings*

Favorite recipe from **Florida Department of Agriculture and Consumer Services, Bureau of Seafood and Aquaculture**

Cellophane Noodles with Minced Pork

    1 package (about 4 ounces) cellophane noodles (bean threads)
   32 dried shiitake mushrooms
    2 tablespoons minced fresh ginger
    2 tablespoons black bean sauce
 1 1/2 cups chicken broth
    1 tablespoon rice wine or dry sherry
    1 tablespoon soy sauce
    2 tablespoons vegetable oil
    6 ounces lean ground pork
    3 green onions, sliced
    1 small jalapeño pepper,* seeded and finely chopped
      Chopped fresh cilantro and hot red pepper slices (optional)
      Green onion slivers (optional)

Jalapeños can sting and irritate the skin; wear rubber or plastic gloves when handling and do not touch eyes. Wash hands after handling.

1. Place cellophane noodles and dried mushrooms in separate bowls; cover each with hot water. Let stand 30 minutes; drain. Cut noodles into 4-inch pieces.

2. Squeeze out excess water from mushrooms. Cut off and discard mushroom stems; cut caps into thin slices.

3. Combine ginger and black bean sauce; set aside. Combine chicken broth, rice wine and soy sauce; set aside.

4. Heat oil in wok or large skillet over high heat. Add pork; stir-fry 2 minutes or until cooked through. Add green onions, jalapeño pepper and black bean sauce mixture. Stir-fry 1 minute.

5. Add chicken broth mixture, noodles and mushrooms. Simmer, uncovered, 5 minutes or until most of the liquid is absorbed. Garnish with cilantro, peppers and green onion slivers.   *Makes 4 servings*

Cellophane Noodles with Minced Pork

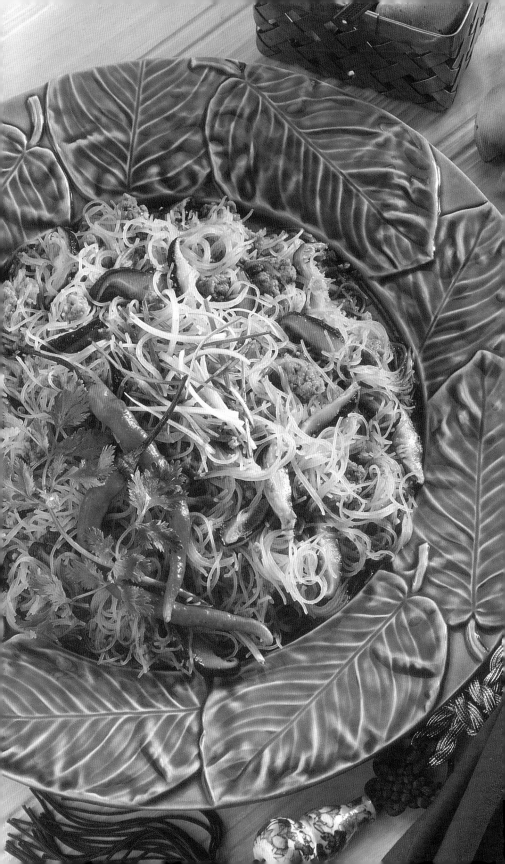

Szechuan Pork Stir-Fry over Spinach

2 teaspoons dark sesame oil, divided

¾ cup matchstick-size carrot strips

8 ounces pork tenderloin, thinly sliced, slices halved

3 cloves garlic, minced

2 teaspoons minced fresh ginger

¼ to ½ teaspoon crushed red pepper flakes

1 tablespoon rice wine or dry sherry

1 tablespoon soy sauce

2 teaspoons cornstarch

8 ounces baby spinach

2 teaspoons sesame seeds, toasted

1. Heat 1 teaspoon oil in large nonstick skillet over medium-high heat. Add carrot strips. Cook 3 minutes, stirring occasionally. Add pork, garlic, ginger and red pepper flakes. Stir-fry 3 minutes or until pork is no longer pink. Stir rice wine and soy sauce into cornstarch in small bowl. Add to pork mixture. Stir-fry until sauce thickens.

2. Heat remaining 1 teaspoon oil in medium saucepan over medium-high heat. Add spinach. Cover and cook 1 to 2 minutes or until spinach is barely wilted. Transfer spinach to serving plates. Spoon pork mixture over spinach. Sprinkle with sesame seeds. *Makes 2 servings*

Szechuan Pork Stir-Fry over Spinach

Beef and Asparagus Stir-Fry

¾ **cup water**

3 **tablespoons soy sauce**

3 **tablespoons hoisin sauce**

1 **tablespoon cornstarch**

1 **tablespoon peanut or vegetable oil**

1 **pound beef top sirloin steak, cut into thin strips**

1 **teaspoon dark sesame oil**

1 **cup baby corn**

8 **shiitake mushrooms, stems removed and thinly sliced**

8 **ounces asparagus (8 to 10 medium spears), trimmed and cut into 1-inch pieces**

1 **cup sugar snap peas or snow peas**

½ **cup red bell pepper strips**

½ **cup cherry tomato halves (optional)**

1. Whisk together water, soy sauce, hoisin sauce and cornstarch in small bowl; set aside.

2. Heat peanut oil in large skillet or wok over medium-high heat. Add beef; cook and stir 5 to 6 minutes or until still slightly pink. Remove beef to plate with slotted spoon.

3. Add sesame oil, baby corn and mushrooms; cook and stir 2 to 3 minutes or until mushrooms are tender and corn is heated through. Add asparagus, sugar snap peas and bell pepper strips; cook and stir 1 minute or until crisp-tender.

4. Return beef with any juices to skillet. Stir reserved soy sauce mixture; add to skillet. Add tomatoes, if desired. Cook 1 minute or until liquid has thickened, stirring occasionally.   *Makes 4 servings*

Stir-Fried Pork with Green Beans and Baby Corn

¾ **pound pork tenderloin**

2 **tablespoons soy sauce**

1 **tablespoon rice wine or dry sherry**

1 **teaspoon sugar**

½ **teaspoon dark sesame oil**

1 **tablespoon plus 1 teaspoon cornstarch, divided**

⅓ **cup plus 2 tablespoons water, divided**

2 **tablespoons peanut oil, divided**

1 **pound green beans, cut into 1½-inch pieces**

2 **cloves garlic, minced**

1 **teaspoon finely chopped fresh ginger**

1 **tablespoon black bean sauce**

1 **can (14 ounces) baby corn, rinsed and drained**

1. Slice pork across grain into thin slices; cut slices into ¾-inch strips.

2. Stir soy sauce, rice wine, sugar and sesame oil into 1 teaspoon cornstarch in medium bowl; mix well. Add pork; toss to coat. Set aside to marinate 20 to 30 minutes. Stir ⅓ cup water into remaining 1 tablespoon cornstarch in small bowl; set aside.

3. Heat 1 tablespoon peanut oil in wok or large skillet over high heat. Add green beans; stir-fry about 4 minutes. Add remaining 2 tablespoons water; reduce heat to medium-low. Cover and simmer 10 to 12 minutes or until crisp-tender. Remove from wok; set aside.

4. Heat remaining 1 tablespoon peanut oil in wok over high heat. Add garlic, ginger and pork; stir-fry about 3 minutes or until meat is no longer pink. Add black bean sauce; stir-fry 1 minute.

5. Return beans to wok. Stir cornstarch mixture; add to wok. Bring to a boil; cook until sauce thickens. Stir in baby corn; heat through.

Makes 4 servings

Stir-Fried Pork with Green Beans and Baby Corn

Seafood Specialties

Szechuan Tuna Steaks

4 tuna steaks (6 ounces each), cut 1 inch thick
¼ cup rice wine or dry sherry
¼ cup soy sauce
1 tablespoon dark sesame oil
1 teaspoon hot chili oil *or* ¼ teaspoon red pepper flakes
1 clove garlic, minced
3 tablespoons chopped fresh cilantro

1. Place tuna in single layer in large shallow glass dish. Combine rice wine, soy sauce, sesame oil, hot chili oil and garlic in small bowl. Reserve ¼ cup soy sauce mixture at room temperature. Pour remaining soy sauce mixture over tuna. Cover; marinate in refrigerator 40 minutes, turning once.

2. Spray grid with nonstick cooking spray. Prepare grill for direct grilling.

3. Drain tuna, discarding marinade. Place tuna on grid. Grill, uncovered, over medium-hot coals 6 minutes or until tuna is seared, but still feels somewhat soft in center,* turning halfway through grilling time. Transfer tuna to carving board. Cut each tuna steak into thin slices; fan out slices onto serving plates. Drizzle with reserved soy sauce mixture; sprinkle with cilantro.

Makes 4 servings

Tuna becomes dry and tough if overcooked. Cook it to medium doneness for best results.

Grilled Chinese Salmon

3 tablespoons soy sauce

2 tablespoons rice wine or dry sherry

2 cloves garlic, minced

1 pound salmon fillets or steaks

2 tablespoons finely chopped fresh cilantro

1. Combine soy sauce, sherry and garlic in shallow dish. Add salmon; turn to coat. Cover; refrigerate at least 30 minutes or up to 2 hours.

2. Preheat broiler or grill. Remove salmon from dish; reserve marinade. Arrange fillets skin side down on oiled rack of broiler pan or oiled grid over hot coals. Broil or grill 5 to 6 inches from heat 10 minutes or until fish begins to flake when tested with fork. Baste with reserved marinade after 5 minutes of broiling; discard any remaining marinade. Sprinkle with cilantro.

Makes 4 servings

Chinese rice wine is a mildly alcoholic brew made from fermenting sticky (glutinous) white rice. It is slightly sweet, has a golden color and is sometimes referred to as "yellow wine." Rice wine is frequently used in Chinese marinades where it provides acidity in the same way a vinegar or grape wine would. It should be stored at room temperature, tightly sealed and out of the sunlight. Pale dry sherry may be substituted for Chinese rice wine. Sake is a Japanese rice wine that could also be substituted but with a sweeter result.

Easy Seafood Stir-Fry

1 package (1 ounce) dried shiitake mushrooms*
$\frac{1}{2}$ cup reduced-sodium chicken broth
2 tablespoons rice wine or dry sherry
1 tablespoon soy sauce
4$\frac{1}{2}$ teaspoons cornstarch
1 teaspoon vegetable oil, divided
$\frac{1}{2}$ pound bay scallops or halved sea scallops
$\frac{1}{4}$ pound medium raw shrimp, peeled and deveined
2 cloves garlic, minced
6 ounces (2 cups) snow peas, cut diagonally in half
2 cups hot cooked white rice
$\frac{1}{4}$ cup thinly sliced green onions

*Or substitute 1$\frac{1}{2}$ cups sliced fresh mushrooms. Omit step 1.

1. Place mushrooms in small bowl; cover with warm water. Soak 20 minutes to soften. Drain; squeeze out excess water. Discard stems; slice caps.

2. Blend broth, rice wine and soy sauce into cornstarch in small bowl until smooth.

3. Heat $\frac{1}{2}$ teaspoon oil in wok or large nonstick skillet over medium heat. Add scallops, shrimp and garlic; stir-fry 3 minutes or until seafood is opaque. Remove and reserve.

4. Add remaining $\frac{1}{2}$ teaspoon oil to wok. Add mushrooms and snow peas; stir-fry 3 minutes or until snow peas are crisp-tender.

5. Stir broth mixture and add to wok. Cook 2 minutes or until sauce boils and thickens. Return seafood and any accumulated juices to wok; heat through. Serve with rice. Sprinkle with green onions.   Makes 4 servings

Beijing Fillet of Sole

  2 tablespoons soy sauce
  2 teaspoons dark sesame oil
  4 sole fillets (6 ounces each)
1 1/4 cups shredded cabbage or coleslaw mix
  1/2 cup crushed chow mein noodles
  1 egg white, lightly beaten
  2 teaspoons sesame seeds
  1 package (10 ounces) frozen snow peas, cooked and drained

1. Preheat oven to 350°F. Combine soy sauce and oil in small bowl. Place sole in shallow dish. Lightly brush both sides of sole with soy sauce mixture.

2. Combine cabbage, noodles, egg white and remaining soy sauce mixture in medium bowl. Spoon evenly over each fillet. Roll up fillets. Place, seam side down, in shallow foil-lined roasting pan.

3. Sprinkle rolls with sesame seeds. Bake 25 to 30 minutes or until fish begins to flake when tested with fork. Serve with snow peas.

Makes 4 servings

Scallops with Vegetables

1 ounce dried shiitake mushrooms
1 cup cold water
4 teaspoons cornstarch
2½ tablespoons rice wine or dry sherry
4 teaspoons soy sauce
2 teaspoons instant chicken bouillon granules
2 tablespoons vegetable oil
8 ounces green beans, cut into 1-inch pieces
2 yellow onions, cut into wedges and separated
3 stalks celery, cut into ½-inch pieces
2 teaspoons minced fresh ginger
1 clove garlic, minced
1 pound sea scallops, cut into quarters if large
6 green onions, cut into thin slices
1 can (15 ounces) baby corn, drained

1. Place mushrooms in bowl; cover with hot water. Let stand 30 minutes; drain. Squeeze out excess moisture. Cut off and discard stems; cut caps into thin slices.

2. Blend cold water into cornstarch in small bowl; stir in rice wine, soy sauce and bouillon granules. Set aside.

3. Heat oil in wok or large skillet over high heat. Add green beans, yellow onions, celery, ginger and garlic; stir-fry 3 minutes.

4. Stir cornstarch mixture; add to wok. Cook and stir until sauce boils and thickens.

5. Add mushrooms, scallops, green onions and baby corn. Cook and stir 4 minutes or until scallops turn opaque.   *Makes 4 to 6 servings*

Broiled Hunan Fish Fillets

3 tablespoons soy sauce
1 tablespoon finely chopped green onion
2 teaspoons dark sesame oil
1 clove garlic, minced
1 teaspoon minced fresh ginger
¼ teaspoon red pepper flakes
1 pound red snapper, scrod or cod fillets

1. Combine soy sauce, green onion, oil, garlic, ginger and red pepper flakes in small bowl.

2. Spray rack of broiler pan with nonstick cooking spray. Place fish on rack; brush with soy sauce mixture.

3. Broil 4 to 5 inches from heat 10 minutes or until fish begins to flake when tested with fork.   *Makes 4 servings*

In Chinese cuisine, fish is considered a greater delicacy than meat or poultry and is treated with great care. It is often served at celebrations and happy occasions. When cooking fish it is important to remember that it will continue to cook after being removed from the heat source. Try to stop the cooking slightly before the fish is done to prevent it from becoming dry and flavorless.

Shrimp in Mock Lobster Sauce

½ **cup reduced-sodium beef or chicken broth**

¼ **cup oyster sauce**

1 **tablespoon cornstarch**

1 **egg**

1 **egg white**

1 **tablespoon peanut or canola oil**

¾ **pound medium or large raw shrimp, peeled and deveined**

2 **cloves garlic, minced**

3 **green onions, cut into ½-inch pieces**

2 **cups hot cooked Chinese egg noodles**

1. Stir broth and oyster sauce into cornstarch in small bowl until smooth. Beat egg with egg white in separate small bowl. Set aside.

2. Heat oil in wok over medium-high heat 1 minute. Add shrimp and garlic; stir-fry 3 to 5 minutes or until shrimp turn pink and opaque.

3. Stir broth mixture; add to wok. Add green onions; stir-fry 1 minute or until sauce boils and thickens.

4. Stir eggs into wok; stir-fry 1 minute or just until eggs are set. Serve over noodles.   *Makes 4 servings*

Note: Oyster sauce is a thick, brown, concentrated sauce made of ground oysters, soy sauce and brine. It imparts a slight fish flavor and is used as a seasoning. It is readily available in the Asian section of large supermarkets.

Szechuan Seafood Stir-Fry

1 package (10 ounces) spinach
4 teaspoons dark sesame oil, divided
4 cloves garlic, minced, divided
¼ cup soy sauce
1 tablespoon rice wine or dry sherry
1 tablespoon cornstarch
1 medium red bell pepper, cut into strips
1½ teaspoons minced fresh ginger
¾ pound large raw shrimp, peeled and deveined
½ pound bay scallops
2 teaspoons sesame seeds, toasted

1. Rinse spinach in cold water; drain. Heat 2 teaspoons oil in large saucepan over medium heat. Add 2 cloves garlic; stir-fry 1 minute. Add spinach; cover and steam 3 to 5 minutes or until spinach is wilted. Keep warm.

2. Meanwhile, stir soy sauce and rice wine into cornstarch until smooth. Heat remaining 2 teaspoons oil in large nonstick skillet over medium-high heat. Add bell pepper; stir-fry 2 minutes. Add remaining 2 cloves garlic and ginger; stir-fry 1 minute. Add shrimp; stir-fry 2 minutes. Add scallops; stir-fry 1 minute or until shrimp and scallops are opaque. Stir reserved soy sauce mixture and add to skillet; stir-fry 1 minute or until sauce thickens.

3. Stir spinach mixture and transfer to 4 plates; top with seafood mixture and sprinkle with sesame seeds. *Makes 4 servings*

Substitution: Substitute one large head bok choy, thinly sliced, for spinach. Increase steaming time to 8 minutes or until bok choy is tender.

Stir-Fried Crab

8 ounces firm tofu, drained
1 tablespoon soy sauce
¼ cup chicken broth
3 tablespoons oyster sauce
2 teaspoons cornstarch
1 tablespoon peanut or vegetable oil
2 cups (6 ounces) snow peas, cut into halves
8 ounces (2 cups) crabmeat or imitation crabmeat, shredded
  Sesame Noodle Cake (recipe follows)
2 tablespoons chopped fresh cilantro or thinly sliced green onions

1. Cut tofu into ½-inch squares or triangles. Place in shallow dish. Drizzle soy sauce over tofu. Blend broth and oyster sauce into cornstarch in small bowl until smooth.

2. Heat oil in wok or large skillet over medium-high heat. Add snow peas; stir-fry 3 minutes or until crisp-tender. Add crabmeat; stir-fry 1 minute. Stir broth mixture and add to wok. Stir-fry 30 seconds or until sauce boils and thickens.

3. Stir in tofu mixture; heat through. Serve over Sesame Noodle Cake. Sprinkle with cilantro.   *Makes 4 servings*

Sesame Noodle Cake

4 ounces cellophane noodles (bean threads) or Chinese egg noodles, cooked and drained
1 tablespoon soy sauce
1 tablespoon peanut or vegetable oil
½ teaspoon dark sesame oil

Toss noodles with soy sauce in large bowl. Heat peanut oil in medium nonstick skillet over medium heat. Add noodles; pat into even layer with spatula. Cook 6 minutes or until bottom is well browned. Drizzle with sesame oil.   *Makes 4 servings*

Stir-Fried Crab
and Sesame Noodle Cake

Steamed Fish Fillets with Black Bean Sauce

1½ pounds white-fleshed fish fillets (Lake Superior whitefish, halibut, rainbow trout or catfish)

1 tablespoon vegetable oil

2 green onions, sliced

2 tablespoons minced fresh ginger

2 tablespoons black bean sauce (see note)

Hot cooked rice (optional)

Green onion slivers (optional)

1. Fill large saucepan about one-third full with water. Place bamboo steamer basket over saucepan. Or, fill wok fitted with rack about one-third full with water. Cover and bring water to a boil. Place fillets in single layer on platter that fits into steamer or wok.

2. Heat oil in small skillet over medium-high heat. Add green onions, ginger and black bean sauce; cook and stir 30 seconds or just until fragrant. Immediately pour contents of skillet evenly over fillets. Place platter in steamer; cover and steam 10 to 15 minutes or until fish begins to flake when tested with fork.

3. Serve fillets and sauce over rice, if desired. Garnish with green onion slivers.

Makes 4 servings

Note: Jarred black bean sauce is sold in the Asian food section of most large supermarkets. It is made of fermented black soybeans, soy sauce, garlic, sherry, sesame oil and ginger. Black soybeans have a pungent odor and a unique, pronounced flavor. Do not substitute regular black beans.

Chinese American

Cantonese Pork

2 pork tenderloins (about 2 pounds)
1 tablespoon vegetable oil
1 can (8 ounces) pineapple chunks in juice, undrained
1 can (8 ounces) tomato sauce
2 cans (4 ounces each) sliced mushrooms, drained
1 medium onion, thinly sliced
3 tablespoons brown sugar
2 tablespoons Worcestershire sauce
1½ teaspoons salt
1½ teaspoons white vinegar
    Hot cooked rice

Slow Cooker Directions

1. Cut tenderloins in half lengthwise, then crosswise into ¼-inch-thick slices. Heat oil in large nonstick skillet over medium-low heat. Brown pork on all sides. Drain and discard fat.

2. Place pork, pineapple with juice, tomato sauce, mushrooms, onion, brown sugar, Worcestershire, salt and vinegar in slow cooker.

3. Cover; cook on LOW 6 to 8 hours or on HIGH 4 hours. Serve over rice. *Makes 8 servings*

Easy Fried Rice

¼ cup BERTOLLI® Olive Oil
4 cups cooked rice
2 cloves garlic, finely chopped
1 envelope LIPTON® RECIPE SECRETS® Onion Mushroom Soup Mix
½ cup water
1 tablespoon soy sauce
1 cup frozen peas and carrots, partially thawed
2 eggs, lightly beaten

1. In 12-inch nonstick skillet, heat olive oil over medium-high heat and cook rice, stirring constantly, 2 minutes or until rice is heated through. Stir in garlic.

2. Stir in soup mix blended with water and soy sauce and cook 1 minute. Stir in peas and carrots and cook 2 minutes or until heated through.

3. Make a well in center of rice and quickly stir in eggs until cooked.

Makes 4 servings

Prep Time: 10 minutes
Cook Time: 10 minutes

It's usually a good idea to make more rice than you will need at one meal when you're preparing it. Extra rice can be refrigerated for several days and used in other recipes. In fact, rice that has been refrigerated works much better than freshly cooked in fried rice recipes because it clumps together less. Rice can also be frozen for up to 3 months. Re-heat by steaming over hot water or defrosting in the microwave.

Easy Fried Rice

Lemon-Orange Glazed Ribs

2 whole slabs baby back pork ribs, cut into halves (about 3 pounds)
2 tablespoons lemon juice
2 tablespoons orange juice
2 tablespoons soy sauce
2 cloves garlic, minced
¼ cup orange marmalade
1 tablespoon hoisin sauce

1. Place ribs in large resealable food storage bag. Combine lemon juice, orange juice, soy sauce and garlic in small bowl; pour over ribs. Close bag securely; turn to coat. Marinate in refrigerator at least 4 hours or up to 24 hours, turning once.

2. Preheat oven to 350°F. Drain ribs; reserve marinade. Place ribs on rack in foil-lined, shallow roasting pan. Brush half of marinade evenly over ribs; bake 20 minutes. Turn ribs over; brush with remaining marinade. Bake 20 minutes.

3. Remove ribs from oven; pour off drippings. Combine marmalade and hoisin sauce in cup; brush half of mixture over ribs. Return to oven; bake 10 minutes or until glazed. Turn ribs over; brush with remaining marmalade mixture. Bake 10 minutes more or until ribs are browned and glazed.

Makes 4 servings

Sweet and Sour Pork

¾ **pound boneless pork**
1 **teaspoon vegetable oil**
1 **bag (16 ounces) BIRDS EYE® frozen Pepper Stir Fry vegetables**
1 **tablespoon water**
1 **jar (14 ounces) sweet and sour sauce**
1 **can (8 ounces) pineapple chunks, drained**

• Cut pork into thin strips.

• In large skillet, heat oil over medium-high heat.

• Add pork; stir-fry until pork is browned.

• Add vegetables and water; cover and cook over medium heat 5 to 7 minutes or until vegetables are crisp-tender.

• Uncover; stir in sweet and sour sauce and pineapple. Cook until heated through. *Makes 4 servings*

Serving Suggestion: Serve over hot cooked rice.

Birds Eye Idea: For a quick sweet and sour sauce for chicken nuggets or egg rolls, add sugar and vinegar to taste to jarred strained apricots or peaches.

Prep Time: 5 minutes
Cook Time: 15 to 18 minutes

Chinese Cashew Chicken

1 pound fresh bean sprouts *or* **1 can (16 ounces) bean sprouts, drained**
2 cups sliced cooked chicken
1 can (10¾ ounces) condensed cream of mushroom soup, undiluted
1 cup sliced celery
½ cup chopped green onions
1 can (4 ounces) sliced mushrooms, drained
3 tablespoons butter
1 tablespoon soy sauce
1 cup whole cashews
   Hot cooked rice

Slow Cooker Directions

1. Combine bean sprouts, chicken, soup, celery, onions, mushrooms, butter and soy sauce in slow cooker; mix well.

2. Cover; cook on LOW 4 to 6 hours or on HIGH 2 to 3 hours.

3. Stir in cashews just before serving. Serve with rice.

Makes 4 servings

Szechuan Grilled Flank Steak

1 beef flank steak (1¼ to 1½ pounds)
¼ cup seasoned rice vinegar
¼ cup soy sauce
2 tablespoons dark sesame oil
4 cloves garlic, minced
2 teaspoons minced fresh ginger
½ teaspoon red pepper flakes
¼ cup water
½ cup thinly sliced green onions
2 to 3 teaspoons sesame seeds, toasted
   Hot cooked rice (optional)

1. Place steak in large resealable food storage bag. Combine vinegar, soy sauce, oil, garlic, ginger and red pepper in small bowl; pour over steak. Press air from bag and seal; turn to coat. Marinate in refrigerator 3 hours, turning once.

2. Spray grid with nonstick cooking spray. Prepare coals for direct grilling. Drain steak, reserving marinade in small saucepan. Place steak on grid over medium heat. Grill, uncovered, 17 to 21 minutes for medium rare to medium (160°F), turning once.

3. Add water to reserved marinade. Bring to a boil over high heat. Reduce heat to low; simmer 5 minutes. Transfer steak to carving board. Slice steak across grain into thin slices. Drizzle steak with boiled marinade. Sprinkle with green onions and sesame seeds. Serve with rice, if desired.

Makes 4 to 6 servings

Sweet and Spicy Chicken Stir-Fry

1½ cups uncooked long-grain white rice
1 can (8 ounces) DEL MONTE® Pineapple Chunks In Its Own Juice
4 boneless, skinless chicken breast halves, cut into bite-size pieces
2 tablespoons vegetable oil
1 large green bell pepper, cut into strips
¾ cup sweet and sour sauce
⅛ to ½ teaspoon red pepper flakes

1. Cook rice according to package directions.

2. Drain pineapple, reserving ⅓ cup juice.

3. Stir-fry chicken in hot oil in large skillet over medium-high heat until no longer pink in center. Add green pepper and reserved pineapple juice; stir-fry 2 minutes or until tender-crisp.

4. Add sweet and sour sauce, red pepper flakes and pineapple; stir-fry 3 minutes or until heated through.

5. Spoon rice onto serving plate; top with chicken mixture. Garnish, if desired.   *Makes 4 servings*

Prep Time: 5 minutes
Cook Time: 20 minutes

Sweet and Spicy Chicken Stir-Fry

Chinese American

Quick 'n' Tangy Beef Stir-Fry

Sauce

- ½ cup *French's®* Worcestershire Sauce
- ½ cup water
- 2 tablespoons sugar
- 2 teaspoons cornstarch
- ½ teaspoon ground ginger
- ½ teaspoon garlic powder

Stir-fry

- 1 pound thinly sliced beef steak
- 3 cups sliced bell peppers

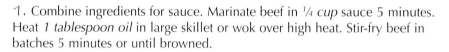

1. Combine ingredients for sauce. Marinate beef in ¼ *cup* sauce 5 minutes. Heat *1 tablespoon oil* in large skillet or wok over high heat. Stir-fry beef in batches 5 minutes or until browned.

2. Add peppers; cook 2 minutes. Add remaining sauce; stir-fry until sauce thickens. Serve over hot cooked ramen noodles or rice, if desired.

Makes 4 servings

Prep Time: 10 minutes
Cook Time: 10 minutes

Easy Make-at-Home Chinese Chicken

3 tablespoons frozen orange juice concentrate

2 tablespoons soy sauce

2 tablespoons water

¾ teaspoon cornstarch

¼ teaspoon garlic powder

   Nonstick cooking spray

2 carrots, cut crosswise into ¼-inch slices

1 package (12 ounces) frozen broccoli and cauliflower florets, thawed

2 teaspoons canola oil

¾ pound boneless skinless chicken breasts, cut into bite-size pieces

1⅓ cups hot cooked rice

1. For sauce, stir together orange juice concentrate, soy sauce, water, cornstarch and garlic powder; set aside.

2. Spray nonstick wok or large skillet with cooking spray. Add carrots; stir-fry over high heat 1 minute. Add broccoli and cauliflower; stir-fry 2 to 3 minutes or until vegetables are crisp-tender. Remove vegetables from wok; set aside.

3. Add oil to wok. Stir-fry chicken in hot oil 2 to 3 minutes or until cooked through. Push chicken up side of wok. Stir sauce and add to wok; cook and stir until thickened. Return vegetables to wok; cook and stir until heated through. Serve over hot cooked rice. *Makes 4 servings*

Tip: To cut carrots decoratively, use a citrus stripper or grapefruit spoon to cut 4 or 5 grooves into whole carrots, cutting lengthwise from stem end to tip. Then cut carrots crosswise into slices.

Easy Make-at-Home Chinese Chicken

One Pan Pork Fu Yung

1 cup reduced-sodium chicken broth
½ teaspoon dark sesame oil, divided
1 tablespoon cornstarch
2 teaspoons canola oil
½ pound boneless pork tenderloin, chopped
5 green onions, thinly sliced, divided
1 cup sliced mushrooms
¼ teaspoon salt
¼ teaspoon white pepper
1 cup bean sprouts
2 eggs
2 egg whites

1. Stir broth and ¼ teaspoon sesame oil into cornstarch in small saucepan. Cook and stir over medium heat about 5 to 6 minutes or until sauce thickens.

2. Heat canola oil in large nonstick skillet over medium-high heat. Add pork; stir-fry 4 minutes or until no longer pink.

3. Reserve 2 tablespoons green onion. Add remaining green onions, ¼ teaspoon sesame oil, mushrooms, salt and white pepper to skillet; stir-fry 4 to 5 minutes or until lightly browned. Add sprouts; stir-fry 1 minute. With spatula, flatten mixture in skillet.

4. Beat eggs and egg whites in medium bowl; pour over pork mixture in skillet. Reduce heat to low. Cover; cook about 3 minutes or until eggs are set.

5. Cut into 4 wedges. Top each wedge with ¼ cup sauce and sprinkle with reserved 2 tablespoons green onion. *Makes 4 servings*

Serving Suggestion: Serve with a lettuce wrap salad. Separate Boston lettuce leaves and arrange on a platter with grated carrot, radish slices, seedless cucumber rounds, red bell pepper strips and bean sprouts. Serve with a dipping sauce made by whisking together 1 cup reduced-sodium chicken broth, 1 tablespoon rice vinegar, ¼ teaspoon dark sesame oil, ¼ teaspoon minced ginger and ¼ teaspoon minced garlic.

Chicken Chow Mein

1 pound boneless skinless chicken breasts, cut into thin strips

2 cloves garlic, minced

1 teaspoon vegetable oil, divided

2 tablespoons rice wine or dry sherry

2 tablespoons soy sauce

2 cups (6 ounces) snow peas, cut into halves

3 green onions, cut into 1-inch pieces

4 ounces uncooked Chinese egg noodles or vermicelli, cooked and drained

1 teaspoon dark sesame oil (optional)

Cherry tomatoes (optional)

Fresh herbs (optional)

1. Toss chicken and garlic in small bowl.

2. Heat ½ teaspoon vegetable oil in wok or large nonstick skillet over medium-high heat. Add chicken mixture; stir-fry 3 minutes or until chicken is cooked through. Transfer to medium bowl; toss with rice wine and soy sauce.

3. Add remaining ½ teaspoon vegetable oil to wok. Add snow peas; stir-fry 1 to 2 minutes or until crisp-tender. Add green onions; stir-fry 30 seconds. Add chicken mixture; stir-fry 1 minute.

4. Add noodles to wok; stir-fry 2 minutes or until heated through. Stir in sesame oil, if desired. Garnish with cherry tomatoes and fresh herbs.

Makes 4 servings

Stir-Fry Tomato Beef

1 cup uncooked long-grain white rice
1 pound flank steak
1 tablespoon cornstarch
1 tablespoon soy sauce
2 cloves garlic, minced
1 teaspoon minced gingerroot *or* **¼ teaspoon ground ginger**
1 tablespoon vegetable oil
1 can (14½ ounces) DEL MONTE® Stewed Tomatoes - Seasoned with Onions, Celery & Green Peppers

1. Cook rice according to package directions.

2. Meanwhile, cut meat in half lengthwise, then cut crosswise into thin slices.

3. Combine cornstarch, soy sauce, garlic and ginger in medium bowl. Add meat; toss to coat.

4. Heat oil in large skillet over high heat. Add meat; cook, stirring constantly, until browned. Add undrained tomatoes; cook until thickened, about 5 minutes, stirring frequently.

5. Serve meat mixture over hot cooked rice. Garnish, if desired.

Makes 4 to 6 servings

Prep Time: 10 minutes
Cook Time: 20 minutes

Contents

It's not surprising that Thai cuisine is an American favorite. Thai food is fresh-tasting, healthy and easy to love. The good news is that creating Thai favorites in an ordinary home kitchen is easy with the recipes in this book. No special equipment is needed, just a deep skillet or wok, a broiler or grill, and the usual saucepans, knives and cutting boards. In fact, in Thailand many cooks turn out an amazing variety of delicious dishes over a simple charcoal fire.

pg.142

Thai cooking is about freshness of ingredients and balance of flavors. Each dish must have the right combination of four primary tastes: sweet, sour, hot and salty. While there are basic rules for balancing the seasoning of a green curry or a satay, most Thai recipes also suggest that you "season according to your heart's desire." It is not only acceptable, but desirable, to adjust the level of heat from chilies or the saltiness from fish sauce to taste. In fact, the only "authentic" approach is one that pleases your palate.

If you lived in Thailand you could purchase freshly made curry pastes, coconut milk and rice noodles at an open-air marketplace. Fortunately, most American supermarkets now stock jarred curry paste, canned coconut milk and dried rice noodles. More exotic items can be purchased at Asian markets or even on-line.

RICE REIGNS SUPREME

Thai meals are usually composed of many small, flavorful dishes served with what is considered the centerpiece of the meal—rice. It is impossible to overestimate the importance of rice to Thai cuisine. The most common expression for eat is "kin khâo" or "eat rice," and the phrase "Have you eaten rice yet?" is a favorite Thai greeting.

Thailand's most famous rice is long-grain jasmine. It is also called fragrant rice because of its delightful, flowery scent. Imported Thai jasmine rice is frequently available in the Asian section of supermarkets and there are even some American-grown versions. Of course, any long-grain rice can be substituted, but you owe it to yourself to at try the real thing at least once.

Secrets to Perfect Rice

1. Use Very Low Heat. If you don't have a burner that holds a low simmer, invest in a device called a heat diffuser or "flame tamer." This round perforated metal disc rests right on the burner, under the saucepan to keep the heat even.

2. Don't Peek! Once the saucepan is covered, don't open it until the cooking time is up. Even a small loss of heat can make a real difference.

3. Invest in a Rice Cooker. Most Asian cooks use one. Rice cookers not only turn out perfect rice every time, most will keep it warm for you, too.

Thai Ingredients

basil: Thai basil has an anise-mint flavor and purple stems, but ordinary sweet basil is quite close in flavor and a good substitute.

bean sprouts: The crisp, delicate sprouts of mung beans are extremely perishable. Purchase sprouts that have their buds attached and that smell and look fresh. Use them within a few days.

cellophane noodles: These clear thin noodles, sold in tangled bunches, are also called bean threads or glass noodles. They are made from mung bean flour and must be soaked before using.

chili peppers: The Thai bird's-eye pepper is a small red chili that packs more heat than any other pepper except the habanero. Serrano or jalapeño peppers are fine substitutes.

Dried red chili peppers are even hotter than fresh ones. Many recipes in this book call for dried red pepper flakes instead, as they are easier to find.

Fresh or dried, chili peppers can sting and irritate the skin. Wear rubber gloves when handling peppers and do not touch your eyes. Be sure to wash your hands and all surfaces and utensils that have been in contact with the peppers after handling.

coconut milk: Unsweetened canned coconut milk is available in the ethnic sections of most supermarkets. Do not confuse it with cream of coconut which is a sweetened product used in drinks like piña coladas. Nor is coconut milk the liquid inside a coconut (that's coconut water).

curry pastes: Most curry pastes include chili peppers, lemongrass, shallots, garlic, ginger, coriander and cumin. Generally green is hotter than red. There are as many recipes as there are Thai cooks! It's best to start by adding less curry paste than the recipe directs, since heat levels vary considerably.

fish sauce: This condiment is used in Southeast Asian cooking as soy sauce is in Chinese cuisine. Don't be put off by its funky aroma which diminishes with cooking. Fish sauce helps balance and complete many dishes.

lemongrass: The flowery perfume of lemongrass is one of the most delightful elements of Thai cooking. To use fresh lemongrass, cut off the moist portion at the root end. Throw away the dry, fibrous stalk and the outer leaves. The tender white portion may then be minced and used. Lemongrass freezes well. Grated lemon peel may be substituted, but with a substantial difference in flavor.

rice noodles: These semi-translucent dried noodles come in many sizes and have many names, including rice stick noodles, rice-flour noodles and pho noodles. Widths range from string thin (usually called rice vermicelli) to 1 inch wide. All rice noodles must be soaked or boiled before using and all may be used interchangeably provided soaking and cooking times are adjusted.

rice papers: Look for packages containing stacks of thin translucent rounds, 6 to 8 inches in diameter, in Asian markets. Rice papers look incredibly fragile, but are actually fairly easy to handle. After soaking they become soft, flexible and a bit stretchy.

Wraps & Appetizers

Thai Salad Rolls with Spicy Sweet & Sour Sauce

Spicy Sweet & Sour Sauce (recipe follows)
3 ounces thin rice noodles (rice vermicelli)
4 ounces large raw shrimp, peeled and deveined
1 medium cucumber, peeled, seeded and cut into matchstick-size strips
½ cup fresh cilantro leaves
½ cup fresh mint leaves
1 large bunch green leaf lettuce or Boston bibb lettuce

1. Prepare Spicy Sweet & Sour Sauce; set aside. Soak noodles in hot water 10 minutes to soften. Rinse under cold running water to cool; drain.

2. Meanwhile, bring water to a boil in medium saucepan. Add shrimp; return to a boil. Cook 3 to 5 minutes or until shrimp turn pink and opaque; drain. When cool, cut each shrimp lengthwise in half.

3. To assemble rolls, arrange shrimp, noodles, cucumber, cilantro and mint in center of lettuce leaves and roll up. Serve with Spicy Sweet & Sour Sauce.   *Makes 6 servings*

continued on page 102

Thai Salad Rolls with Spicy Sweet & Sour Sauce, continued

Spicy Sweet & Sour Sauce

1 green onion
2 tablespoons rice vinegar
1 tablespoon cornstarch
¾ cup water
¼ cup packed brown sugar
½ teaspoon red pepper flakes
2 tablespoons finely grated turnip

1. Finely chop white part of green onion; cut green portion into thin, 1-inch strips. Reserve green strips for garnish.

2. Combine vinegar and cornstarch in small bowl; mix well. Set aside.

3. Combine water, brown sugar, red pepper flakes and chopped green onion in small saucepan; bring to a boil. Stir cornstarch mixture; add to saucepan. Return to a boil; cook 1 minute or until sauce thickens. Cool. Sprinkle with turnip and reserved green onion strips just before serving.

Makes about 1 cup

There are many different kinds of rice vinegar used in Asian cuisine. Both Japanese and Chinese rice vinegar are made from fermented rice. They are milder and less acidic than ordinary white vinegar. Seasoned rice vinegar is a Japanese vinegar flavored with salt and sugar and often used to prepare sushi rice. Chinese black vinegar is used mainly as a table condiment. It has a slightly sweet flavor similar to balsamic vinegar.

Chicken Kabobs with Thai Dipping Sauce

1 pound boneless skinless chicken breasts, cut into 1-inch cubes
1 small cucumber, seeded and cut into small chunks
1 cup cherry tomatoes
2 green onions, cut into 1-inch pieces
²/₃ cup teriyaki baste & glaze sauce
¹/₃ cup *Frank's® RedHot® Original Cayenne Pepper Sauce*
¹/₃ cup peanut butter
3 tablespoons frozen orange juice concentrate, undiluted
2 cloves garlic, minced

Thread chicken, cucumber, tomatoes and onions alternately onto metal skewers; set aside.

To prepare Thai Dipping Sauce, combine teriyaki baste & glaze sauce, **Frank's RedHot** Sauce, peanut butter, orange juice concentrate and garlic; mix well. Reserve ²/₃ cup sauce for dipping.

Brush skewers with some of remaining sauce. Place skewers on oiled grid. Grill over hot coals 10 minutes or until chicken is no longer pink in center, turning and basting often with remaining sauce. Serve skewers with reserved Thai Dipping Sauce. Garnish as desired.

Makes 6 appetizer servings

Prep Time: 15 minutes
Cook Time: 10 minutes

Thai Lamb & Couscous Rolls

16 large napa cabbage leaves, stems trimmed
 1 cup water
 2 tablespoons minced fresh ginger
 1 teaspoon red pepper flakes
²/₃ cup uncooked couscous
   Nonstick cooking spray
½ pound lean ground lamb
½ cup chopped green onions
 3 cloves garlic, minced
¼ cup plus 2 tablespoons minced fresh cilantro or mint, divided
 2 tablespoons soy sauce
 1 tablespoon lime juice
 1 teaspoon dark sesame oil
 1 cup plain yogurt

1. Fill large saucepan two-thirds full with water; bring to a boil over high heat. Drop cabbage leaves into water; cook 30 seconds. Drain. Rinse under cold water until cool; pat dry with paper towels.

2. Place 1 cup water, ginger and red pepper flakes in medium saucepan; bring to a boil over high heat. Stir in couscous; cover. Remove saucepan from heat; let stand 5 minutes.

3. Spray large skillet with cooking spray; add lamb, green onions and garlic. Cook and stir over medium-high heat 5 minutes or until lamb is no longer pink. Remove lamb mixture from skillet; drain in colander.

4. Combine couscous, lamb mixture, ¼ cup cilantro, soy sauce, lime juice and oil in medium bowl. Spoon mixture evenly down centers of cabbage leaves. Fold ends of cabbage leaves over filling; roll up. Combine yogurt and remaining 2 tablespoons cilantro in small bowl; spoon evenly over rolls. Serve warm.   *Makes 16 servings*

Crisp Fish Cakes

Ginger Dipping Sauce (recipe follows)
1 pound boneless catfish, halibut or cod fillets, cut into 1-inch pieces
1 tablespoon fish sauce
3 cloves garlic, minced
1 tablespoon chopped fresh cilantro
2 teaspoons grated lemon peel
1 teaspoon minced fresh ginger
1/8 teaspoon ground red pepper
Peanut oil for frying
1 head curly leaf lettuce
1 medium green or red apple, cut into thin strips *or* 1 ripe mango, diced
1/2 cup fresh cilantro leaves
1/3 cup fresh mint leaves

1. Prepare Ginger Dipping Sauce; set aside.

2. Process fish pieces in food processor 10 to 20 seconds or just until coarsely chopped. *Do not purée.* Add fish sauce, garlic, chopped cilantro, lemon peel, ginger and red pepper; process 5 seconds or until combined.

3. Rub cutting board with 1 to 2 teaspoons peanut oil. Place fish mixture on board; pat evenly into 7-inch square. Cut into 16 squares; shape each square into 2-inch patty.

4. Heat 1 to 1½ inches oil in Dutch oven or large skillet over medium-high heat until oil registers 360°F to 375°F on deep-fry thermometer. Place patties on slotted spoon and lower into hot oil.

5. Fry patties in batches 2 to 3 minutes or until golden and opaque in center. (Do not crowd pan. Allow oil to return to temperature between batches.) Remove with slotted spoon to paper towels; drain.

continued on page 108

Crisp Fish Cakes

Crisp Fish Cakes, continued

6. Serve with lettuce leaves, apple, cilantro leaves, mint leaves and Ginger Dipping Sauce. To eat, stack 1 fish cake, apple strips, cilantro and mint in center of lettuce leaf. Drizzle with sauce; enclose filling in lettuce leaf.

Makes 6 to 8 servings

Ginger Dipping Sauce

- ¼ **cup rice vinegar**
- 2 **tablespoons water**
- 1 **teaspoon sugar**
- 1 **teaspoon minced fresh ginger**
- ½ **teaspoon red pepper flakes**
- ½ **teaspoon fish sauce**

Combine all ingredients in small bowl; stir until sugar dissolves.

Makes about ⅓ cup

Spicy Thai Satay Dip

- ⅓ **cup peanut butter**
- ⅓ **cup** *French's®* **Honey Dijon Mustard**
- ⅓ **cup fat-free chicken broth**
- 1 **tablespoon chopped peeled fresh ginger**
- 1 **tablespoon honey**
- 1 **tablespoon** *Frank's® RedHot®* **Cayenne Pepper Sauce**
- 1 **tablespoon teriyaki sauce**
- 1 **tablespoon grated orange peel**
- 2 **cloves garlic, minced**

1. Combine all ingredients in large bowl. Cover and refrigerate.

2. Serve with vegetables, chips or grilled meats.

Makes 4 (¼-cup) servings

Prep Time: 10 minutes

Spicy Thai Satay Dip

Thai Summer Rolls

Thai Dipping Sauce (page 112)
8 ounces medium raw shrimp, peeled and deveined
3½ ounces thin rice noodles (rice vermicelli)
12 rice paper wrappers,* about 6½ inches in diameter
36 fresh cilantro leaves
4 ounces roast pork or beef, sliced ⅛ inch thick
1 tablespoon chopped peanuts
Lime peel (optional)

* Rice paper is a thin, edible wrapper used in Southeast Asian cooking.

1. Prepare Thai Dipping Sauce; set aside.

2. Bring large saucepan of water to a boil over high heat. Add shrimp; simmer 1 to 2 minutes or until shrimp turn pink and opaque. Remove shrimp with slotted spoon to small bowl. When cool, slice shrimp in half lengthwise.

3. Meanwhile, soften rice noodles in medium bowl of hot water 20 to 30 minutes or according to package directions. Drain; cut noodles into manageable 3-inch lengths.

4. Soften rice paper wrappers in large bowl of warm water 30 to 40 seconds or until pliable. Drain wrappers, 1 at a time, on paper towels and transfer to clean work surface. Arrange 3 cilantro leaves in center of wrapper. Layer with two shrimp halves, some pork and rice noodles.

5. Fold bottom of wrapper up over filling; fold in each side and roll up, burrito-style. Repeat with remaining filling and wrappers.

6. Sprinkle rolls with peanuts. Serve with Thai Dipping Sauce. Garnish with lime peel.

Makes 12 summer rolls

continued on page 112

Thai Summer Rolls

Thai Summer Rolls, continued

Thai Dipping Sauce

½ **cup water**
¼ **cup fish sauce**
2 **tablespoons lime juice**
1 **tablespoon sugar**
1 **clove garlic, minced**
¼ **teaspoon chili oil**

Combine all ingredients in small bowl; mix well.   *Makes about 1 cup*

*Rice papers look incredibly fragile, but are actually fairly easy to work
with, once you get the knack. After soaking they become soft, flexible and
a bit stretchy. You can allow everyone at the dinner table to assemble their
own summer rolls instead of doing it ahead of time if you like. Just set out
the assorted fillings and provide softened rice papers for a do-it-yourself
Thai appetizer.*

Thai Chicken & Pear Lettuce Wraps

1 can (15 ounces) Bartlett pear slices or halves
4 cups diced cooked chicken
1 cup salted peanut halves
1 cup sliced green onion
2 tablespoons tablespoons minced cilantro
1 tablespoon Thai fish sauce* (or olive oil)**
1 teaspoon brown sugar
1 tablespoon lime or lemon juice
2 serrano chiles, seeded and minced
9 to 10 head lettuce or leaf lettuce leaves

Thai fish sauce (nam pla) is available in the Asian section of larger supermarkets or Asian markets.

**If you substitute olive oil for the Thai fish sauce, you will have a different, but still delicious, salad dressing.*

Drain pears, reserving 2 tablespoons of the juice. Dice pears. In a bowl toss together pears, chicken, peanuts, green onion and cilantro. In a small bowl whisk together Thai fish sauce or olive oil, sugar, reserved pear juice, lime juice and chiles. Pour dressing over chicken mixture. Cover and chill several hours or overnight. To serve, spoon about $1/3$ cup of the mixture onto a lettuce leaf. Fold in sides of lettuce leaf, then roll up like a burrito. Repeat with remaining filling and lettuce leaves. *Makes 3 servings*

Notes: Makes about 4 cups salad mixture. If transporting salad, pack salad and lettuce leaves in separate self-sealing bags or containers; keep chilled until serving.

*Favorite recipe from **Pacific Northwest Canned Pear Service***

Thai Pizza

1 package JENNIE-O TURKEY STORE® Breast Strips
2 teaspoons bottled or fresh minced ginger
2 teaspoons bottled or fresh minced garlic
¼ teaspoon crushed red pepper flakes
   Cooking spray
¼ cup hoisin or stir-fry sauce
1 large (12-inch) prepared pizza crust
⅓ cup thinly sliced green onions
½ teaspoon finely grated lime peel
⅓ cup coarsely chopped roasted peanuts
2 tablespoons chopped cilantro or basil

Heat oven to 450°F. Toss turkey strips with ginger, garlic and pepper flakes. Coat large nonstick skillet with cooking spray; heat over medium-high heat. Add turkey; stir-fry 2 minutes. Add hoisin sauce; stir-fry 2 minutes. Place pizza crust on large cookie sheet. Spread mixture evenly over pizza crust; sprinkle with green onions and lime peel. Bake 8 to 10 minutes or until crust is golden brown and hot. Sprinkle with peanuts and cilantro. Cut into wedges.

Makes 6 main-dish or 12 appetizer servings

Prep Time: 15 minutes
Cook Time: 15 minutes

Thai Pizza

Salads & Sides

Thai Peanut Salad

1 cup picante sauce
¼ cup chunky-style peanut butter
2 tablespoons honey
2 tablespoons orange juice
1 teaspoon soy sauce
½ teaspoon ground ginger
2 cups (12 ounces) chopped HORMEL® CURE 81® ham
1 (7-ounce) package spaghetti, cooked
¼ cup dry roasted unsalted peanuts
¼ cup red bell pepper, cut into julienne strips
2 tablespoons chopped cilantro

In small saucepan, combine picante sauce, peanut butter, honey, orange juice, soy sauce and ginger. Cook, stirring over low heat until mixture is smooth. Add ¼ cup sauce mixture to ham. Gently toss remaining sauce mixture with hot cooked pasta. Toss pasta mixture with ham mixture, peanuts and pepper strips. Cover and chill 1 to 2 hours. Before serving, sprinkle with cilantro.

Makes 4 servings

Butternut Squash in Coconut Milk

⅓ cup sweetened flaked coconut

2 teaspoons vegetable oil

½ small onion, finely chopped

2 cloves garlic, minced

1 cup unsweetened coconut milk

¼ cup packed brown sugar

1 tablespoon fish sauce

⅛ to ¼ teaspoon red pepper flakes

1 butternut squash (about 2 pounds), peeled and cut into large cubes

1 tablespoon chopped fresh cilantro

1. Preheat oven to 350°F. Spread coconut in baking pan. Bake 6 minutes or until golden, stirring occasionally. Set aside to cool and crisp.

2. Heat oil in large saucepan over medium-high heat. Add onion and garlic; cook and stir 3 minutes or until tender. Add coconut milk, brown sugar, fish sauce and red pepper flakes; stir until sugar is dissolved.

3. Bring mixture to a boil; add squash. Reduce heat to medium; cover and simmer 30 minutes or until squash is tender. Transfer squash to serving bowl with slotted spoon.

4. Increase heat to high; boil remaining liquid until thick, stirring constantly. Pour liquid over squash in bowl. Sprinkle with toasted coconut and chopped cilantro. *Makes 4 to 6 servings*

Thai Grilled Beef Salad

3 tablespoons Thai seasoning, divided

1 beef flank steak (about 1 pound)

2 tablespoons chopped fresh cilantro

2 tablespoons chopped fresh basil

2 Thai chili peppers *or* 1 jalapeño pepper,* seeded and sliced into thin slivers

1 tablespoon finely chopped lemongrass

1 tablespoon minced red onion

1 clove garlic, minced

Juice of 1 lime

1 tablespoon fish sauce

1 large carrot, grated

1 cucumber, chopped

4 cups assorted salad greens

Thai chili peppers and jalapeño peppers can sting and irritate the skin, so wear rubber gloves when handling peppers and do not touch your eyes.

1. Prepare grill for direct cooking.

2. Sprinkle 1 tablespoon Thai seasoning over beef; turn to coat. Cover and marinate 15 minutes. Place steak on grid over medium heat. Grill, uncovered, 17 to 21 minutes for medium rare to medium (160°F), turning once. Cool 10 minutes.

3. Meanwhile, combine remaining 2 tablespoons Thai seasoning, cilantro, basil, chili peppers, lemongrass, red onion, garlic, lime juice and fish sauce in medium bowl; mix well.

4. Thinly slice beef across grain. Add beef, carrot and cucumber to dressing; toss to coat. Arrange on bed of greens.   *Makes 4 servings*

Note: Thai seasoning usually includes chili peppers, garlic, ginger, coriander, lime and basil.

Thai Noodle Soup

1 package (3 ounces) ramen noodles
12 ounces chicken tenders
2 cans (about 14 ounces each) chicken broth
¼ cup shredded carrot
¼ cup snow peas
2 tablespoons thinly sliced green onion
½ teaspoon minced garlic
¼ teaspoon ground ginger
3 tablespoons chopped fresh cilantro
½ lime, cut into 4 wedges

1. Break noodles into pieces. Cook noodles according to package directions; discard flavor packet. Drain; set aside.

2. Cut chicken into ½-inch pieces. Combine chicken broth and chicken in large saucepan or Dutch oven; bring to a boil over medium heat. Cook 2 minutes.

3. Add carrot, snow peas, green onions, garlic and ginger. Reduce heat to low; simmer 3 minutes. Add cooked noodles and cilantro; heat through. Serve soup with lime wedges.   *Makes 4 servings*

Prep and Cook Time: 15 minutes

tip

When purchasing cilantro, look for bright green leaves with no signs of yellowing or wilting. To keep cilantro fresh longer, place the stem ends in a glass of water (like a bouquet), cover loosely with a plastic bag and refrigerate. Wash and chop the herb just before using.

Spinach and Mushroom Stir-Fry

2 tablespoons peanut oil

2 cloves garlic, minced

1 teaspoon minced fresh ginger

¼ to ½ teaspoon red pepper flakes

1 red bell pepper, cut into 1-inch triangles

4 ounces sliced shiitake or button mushrooms*

10 ounces spinach, stemmed and coarsely chopped

1 teaspoon fish sauce

*Or, substitute 1 ounce dried mushrooms, soaked according to package directions.

Heat oil in wok over high heat 1 minute. Add garlic, ginger and red pepper flakes; stir-fry 30 seconds. Add bell pepper and mushrooms; stir-fry 2 minutes. Add spinach and fish sauce; stir-fry 1 to 2 minutes or until spinach is wilted.

Makes 4 servings

Bangkok Rice and Shrimp Salad

½ cup canned coconut milk

¼ cup rice vinegar

1 tablespoon oil

½ teaspoon salt

3 tablespoons chopped fresh basil, plus additional basil leaves for garnish

3 cups cooked U.S. jasmine or medium grain rice

1 pound frozen cooked shrimp, peeled, deveined, thawed

½ cup chopped salted peanuts

Whisk coconut milk, vinegar and oil together in a small bowl. Add salt and basil; set aside. Stir rice, shrimp and coconut milk mixture in medium bowl until blended. Spoon into serving bowl; sprinkle with peanuts and basil to garnish.

Makes 6 servings

*Favorite recipe from **USA Rice***

Thai Chicken Broccoli Salad

4 ounces uncooked linguine
  Nonstick cooking spray
½ pound boneless skinless chicken breasts, cut into 2×½-inch pieces
2 cups broccoli florets
2 tablespoons cold water
⅔ cup chopped red bell pepper
6 green onions, sliced diagonally into 1-inch pieces
¼ cup creamy peanut butter
2 tablespoons hot water
2 tablespoons soy sauce
2 teaspoons dark sesame oil
½ teaspoon red pepper flakes
⅛ teaspoon garlic powder
¼ cup unsalted peanuts, chopped

1. Cook pasta according to package directions. Drain; set aside.

2. Spray large nonstick skillet with cooking spray; heat over medium-high heat. Add chicken; stir-fry 5 minutes or until chicken is cooked through. Remove chicken from skillet.

3. Add broccoli and cold water to skillet. Cook, covered, 2 minutes. Uncover; cook and stir 2 minutes or until broccoli is crisp-tender. Remove broccoli from skillet. Combine pasta, chicken, broccoli, bell pepper and green onions in large bowl.

4. Combine peanut butter, hot water, soy sauce, oil, red pepper flakes and garlic powder in small bowl until well blended. Drizzle over pasta mixture; toss to coat. Top with peanuts before serving.   *Makes 4 servings*

Shrimp, Mushroom and Omelet Soup

10 to 12 dried shiitake mushrooms (about 1 ounce)
3 eggs
1 tablespoon chopped fresh chives or minced green onion tops
2 teaspoons vegetable oil
3 cans (about 14 ounces each) reduced-sodium chicken broth
2 tablespoons oyster sauce
12 ounces medium raw shrimp, peeled and deveined
3 cups lightly packed stemmed spinach leaves
1 tablespoon lime juice
Red pepper flakes

1. Place mushrooms in bowl; cover with hot water. Let stand 30 minutes or until soft. Meanwhile, beat eggs and chives in small bowl.

2. Heat oil in large nonstick skillet over medium-high heat. Pour egg mixture into pan. Reduce heat to medium; cover and cook, without stirring, 2 minutes or until set on bottom. Slide spatula under omelet; lift omelet and tilt pan to allow uncooked egg to flow under. Repeat at several places around omelet.

3. Slide omelet onto flat plate. Hold another plate over omelet and turn omelet over. Slide omelet back into pan to cook other side about 20 seconds. Slide back onto plate. When cool enough to handle, roll up omelet. Slice into $1/4$-inch-wide strips.

4. Drain mushrooms; squeeze out excess water. Remove and discard stems. Slice caps into thin strips.

5. Combine mushrooms, chicken broth and oyster sauce in large saucepan. Cover and bring to a boil over high heat. Reduce heat to low; cook 5 minutes. Increase heat to medium-high; add shrimp. Cook 2 minutes or until shrimp turn pink and opaque. Add omelet strips and spinach; remove from heat. Cover and let stand 1 to 2 minutes or until spinach wilts slightly. Stir in lime juice. Ladle soup into bowls. Sprinkle with red pepper flakes.

Makes 6 servings

Shrimp, Mushroom and Omelet Soup

Thai-Style Salad with Shredded Glazed Chicken

1 head Napa cabbage or romaine lettuce, shredded (about 6 cups)
1 medium cucumber, peeled, halved lengthwise, seeded and sliced (about 1¼ cups)
2 medium carrots, coarsely grated (about 1 cup)
2 small oranges, peeled and cut into segments
½ cup fresh cilantro leaves (optional)
2 Honey-Lime Glazed Chicken Breasts, shredded (recipe follows)
  Honey-Lime Dressing (recipe follows)
¼ cup dry-roasted peanuts, chopped

Combine all ingredients except Honey-Lime Dressing and peanuts in large bowl; toss until well blended. Pour Honey-Lime Dressing over salad; toss until well blended. Sprinkle each serving with peanuts just before serving.

Makes 4 servings

Honey-Lime Dressing: Whisk together 6 tablespoons honey, 3 tablespoons peanut butter, 3 tablespoons lime juice, 2 tablespoons chopped fresh mint, 1 tablespoon minced seeded jalapeño pepper, 1½ teaspoons soy sauce, 1 teaspoon minced garlic and ¾ teaspoon grated lime peel in small bowl until well blended.

*Favorite recipe from **National Honey Board***

Honey-Lime Glazed Chicken

½ cup honey
2 tablespoons lime juice
2 tablespoons chopped fresh cilantro
1 tablespoon soy sauce
2 teaspoons seeded, minced jalapeño pepper
1½ teaspoon minced garlic
6 bone-in chicken breast halves (about 3 pounds)

continued on page 132

Thai-Style Salad with Shredded Glazed Chicken

Thai-Style Salad with Shredded Glazed Chicken, continued

Combine all ingredients except chicken in small bowl until well blended. Place chicken in shallow baking dish; pour half of marinade over chicken. Cover and refrigerate 2 hours or overnight. Reserve remaining marinade. Grill chicken over medium-hot coals about 15 minutes, turning and basting with reserved marinade, or until chicken is no longer pink in center. Reserve 2 chicken breasts for use in Thai-Style Salad with Shredded Glazed Chicken.

*Favorite recipe from **National Honey Board***

Thai Coconut Iced Tea

2 jasmine tea bags
2 cups boiling water
1 cup unsweetened coconut milk
4 teaspoons sugar *or* 2 packets sugar substitute, divided

1. Brew 2 cups jasmine tea with boiling water according to package directions; cool to room temperature.

2. Pour ½ cup coconut milk into each glass. Stir 2 teaspoons of sugar into each glass. Add ice; carefully pour half of tea into each glass. Serve immediately. *Makes 2 servings*

Tip: For a more dramatic presentation, gently pour tea over the back of a spoon held close to the surface of the coconut milk in each glass. The tea will pool in a layer on the coconut milk before blending.

Thai Coconut Iced Tea

From the Land

Thai-Style Pork Chops with Cucumber Sauce

3 tablespoons Thai peanut sauce, divided
¼ teaspoon red pepper flakes or more to taste
4 bone-in pork chops (5 ounces each)
1 container (6 ounces) plain yogurt
¼ cup diced unpeeled cucumber
2 tablespoons chopped red onion
2 tablespoons finely chopped fresh mint or cilantro
1 teaspoon sugar

1. Preheat broiler or prepare grill. Combine 2 tablespoons peanut sauce and pepper flakes; brush mixture evenly over both sides of pork chops. Let stand while preparing cucumber sauce, or refrigerate up to 4 hours.

2. Combine yogurt, cucumber, red onion, mint and sugar in medium bowl; mix well. Broil chops 4 inches from heat source or grill, covered, over medium coals 4 minutes; turn and cook 3 minutes more or until pork is barely pink in center. Just before removing from heat, baste with remaining 1 tablespoon peanut sauce. Serve chops with cucumber sauce.

Makes 4 servings

Serving suggestion: Serve with steamed broccoli and rice.

Pineapple Basil Chicken Supreme

1 can (8 ounces) pineapple chunks in unsweetened juice
2 teaspoons cornstarch
2 tablespoons peanut oil
3 boneless skinless chicken breasts (about 1 pound), cut into bite-size pieces
2 serrano peppers,* minced
2 cloves garlic, minced
2 green onions, cut into 1-inch pieces
¾ cup roasted unsalted cashews
¼ cup chopped fresh basil
1 tablespoon fish sauce
1 tablespoon soy sauce
Hot cooked rice

Serrano peppers can sting and irritate the skin, so wear rubber gloves when handling peppers and do not touch your eyes.

1. Drain pineapple, reserving juice. Combine reserved juice and cornstarch in small bowl; set aside.

2. Heat oil in wok over high heat 1 minute. Add chicken, peppers and garlic; stir-fry 3 minutes or until chicken is cooked through. Add green onions; stir-fry 1 minute. Stir cornstarch mixture; add to wok. Cook 1 minute or until thickened. Add pineapple, cashews, basil, fish sauce and soy sauce; stir-fry 1 minute or until heated through. Serve over rice.   *Makes 4 servings*

Masaman Curry Beef

4 tablespoons vegetable oil, divided
1 medium onion, cut into strips
1½ pounds boneless beef chuck, cut into 1-inch cubes
1 to 2 tablespoons prepared Masaman curry paste
2 cans (about 14 ounces each) unsweetened coconut milk
3 tablespoons fish sauce
2 pounds boiling potatoes, cut into 1½-inch pieces
1 large red bell pepper, cut into strips
½ cup roasted peanuts, chopped
2 tablespoons lime juice
¼ cup slivered fresh basil leaves or chopped fresh cilantro
Hot cooked rice or noodles

1. Heat 1 tablespoon oil in wok or large skillet over medium-high heat. Add onion; stir-fry 6 to 8 minutes or until golden. Transfer onion to bowl with slotted spoon.

2. Add 1 tablespoon oil to wok. Increase heat to high. Add half the beef; stir-fry 2 to 3 minutes until browned on all sides. Transfer beef to another bowl; set aside. Repeat with remaining beef and additional 1 tablespoon oil.

3. Reduce heat to medium. Add remaining 1 tablespoon oil and curry paste to wok; cook and stir 1 to 2 minutes or until fragrant. Add coconut milk and fish sauce; stir to scrape bits of cooked meat and spices from bottom of wok.

4. Return beef to wok. Increase heat to high and bring to a boil. Reduce heat to low; cover and simmer 45 minutes.

5. Add potatoes and return onion to wok. Cook 20 to 30 minutes more or until meat and potatoes are fork-tender. Stir in bell pepper; cook until heated through.

6. Stir in peanuts and lime juice; sprinkle with basil. Serve with rice.

Makes 6 servings

Thai Barbecued Chicken

1 cup coarsely chopped fresh cilantro
2 jalapeño peppers, coarsely chopped
8 cloves garlic, peeled and coarsely chopped
2 tablespoons fish sauce
1 tablespoon packed brown sugar
1 teaspoon curry powder
  Grated peel of 1 lemon
3 pounds chicken pieces

1. Place cilantro, jalapeño peppers, garlic, fish sauce, brown sugar, curry powder and lemon peel in blender or food processor; blend to form coarse paste. Work fingers between skin and meat on breast and thigh pieces. Rub about 1 teaspoon seasoning paste under skin on each piece. Rub chicken pieces on all sides with remaining paste. Place chicken in large resealable food storage bag; marinate in refrigerator 3 to 4 hours or overnight.

2. Prepare grill for direct cooking. Brush grid lightly with oil. Grill chicken over medium coals, skin side down, 10 minutes or until browned. Turn and grill 20 to 30 minutes more or until chicken is cooked through (170°F for breast meat; 180°F for dark meat.)   *Makes 4 servings*

Thai Barbecued Chicken

Thai Duck with Beans and Sprouts

Juice of 1 lime (about 2 tablespoons)

2 tablespoons vegetable oil, divided

2 tablespoons soy sauce

1 tablespoon fish sauce

2 teaspoons minced fresh ginger

2 cloves garlic, minced

1 pound boneless skinless duck breast, cut into ¼-inch strips

1 cup chicken broth

1 tablespoon cornstarch

3 cups green beans

4 green onions, cut into 1-inch pieces

1½ cups bean sprouts

1. Combine lime juice, 1 tablespoon oil, soy sauce, fish sauce, ginger and garlic in medium bowl. Add duck; toss to coat well. Cover and refrigerate 30 minutes to 8 hours.

2. Whisk chicken broth into cornstarch in small bowl; set aside.

3. Heat remaining 1 tablespoon oil in wok or large skillet over high heat. Remove duck from marinade; reserve marinade. Add duck to wok; stir-fry 4 minutes or until no longer pink. Remove duck from wok with slotted spoon.

4. Add green beans to wok; stir-fry 5 to 6 minutes over high heat or until crisp-tender. Add green onions; stir-fry 2 minutes or until crisp-tender. Stir chicken broth mixture; add to wok with reserved marinade. Boil 2 minutes or until sauce thickens. Return duck and accumlated juices to wok. Add bean sprouts; cook and stir until heated through. *Makes 4 servings*

Thai Basil Pork Stir-Fry

1 pound boneless pork tenderloin, cut into ¼-inch slices
½ teaspoon minced garlic
1 tablespoon soy sauce
2 tablespoons canola oil
4 cups broccoli florets
1 medium red bell pepper, cut into strips
1 to 2 tablespoons Thai green curry paste*
1¼ cups chicken broth
2 tablespoons chopped fresh basil
2 tablespoons finely chopped roasted peanuts
3 cups bean sprouts

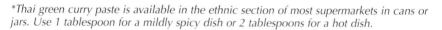

Thai green curry paste is available in the ethnic section of most supermarkets in cans or jars. Use 1 tablespoon for a mildly spicy dish or 2 tablespoons for a hot dish.

1. In a small bowl, combine pork, garlic and soy sauce; toss to coat. Set aside.

2. Heat oil in large nonstick skillet over high heat. Add broccoli; stir-fry 3 to 4 minutes or until broccoli begins to brown but is not cooked through. Add bell pepper; stir-fry 1 minute. Add reserved pork mixture and curry paste; stir-fry 2 minutes more. Add chicken broth; cook and stir 2 to 3 minutes more or until pork is cooked through and vegetables are crisp-tender.

3. Remove from heat; stir in chopped basil.

4. Sprinkle with chopped peanuts and serve with bean sprouts.

Makes 6 servings

Caramelized Lemongrass Chicken

 2 stalks lemongrass
¼ cup sugar
 3 tablespoons fish sauce
 2 cloves garlic, slivered
¼ teaspoon black pepper
1½ pounds skinless chicken thighs (4 to 6 thighs)
 1 tablespoon vegetable oil
 1 tablespoon lemon juice

1. Remove outer leaves from lemongrass and discard. Trim off and discard upper stalks. Flatten lemongrass with meat mallet. Cut lemongrass into 1-inch pieces.

2. Combine sugar, fish sauce, garlic, pepper and lemongrass in large resealable food storage bag; add chicken. Seal bag tightly; turn to coat. Marinate in refrigerator at least 1 hour or up to 4 hours, turning occasionally.

3. Heat oil in large skillet over medium heat. Remove chicken from food storage bag; reserve marinade. Cook chicken 10 minutes or until browned, turning once.

4. Pour reserved marinade into skillet; bring to a boil. Boil 1 to 2 minutes. Reduce heat to low; cover and simmer 30 minutes or until chicken is cooked through (180°F), turning chicken occasionally.

5. Stir lemon juice into skillet. Turn chicken pieces over to coat.

Makes 4 servings

Caramelized Lemongrass Chicken

Swimming Rama

Peanut Sauce (recipe follows)

3 boneless skinless chicken breasts (about 1¼ pounds), sliced crosswise into ½-inch-wide strips

1¾ to 2 pounds spinach, stemmed

1 Thai chili pepper, seeded and finely chopped* *or* ¼ cup diced red bell pepper

*Chili peppers can sting and irritate the skin, so wear rubber gloves when handling peppers and do not touch your eyes.

1. Prepare Peanut Sauce.

2. Bring 6 cups water to a boil in large saucepan over high heat. Add chicken to boiling water; remove saucepan from heat. Let stand, covered, 5 minutes or until chicken is cooked through.

3. Set steamer basket in Dutch oven or large skillet; add water to within ¼ inch of bottom of basket.

4. Bring water to a boil over high heat. Layer about one fourth of spinach in basket; cover and steam 15 seconds. Quickly turn leaves over with tongs. Cover and steam 15 seconds or until leaves are bright green and barely wilted.

5. Transfer spinach to colander. Repeat with remaining spinach. Lay spinach on serving platter or individual plates.

6. Drain chicken; stir into hot Peanut Sauce and pour mixture over spinach. Sprinkle with chili pepper. *Makes 4 servings*

Peanut Sauce

2 teaspoons vegetable oil
½ cup finely chopped onion
3 cloves garlic, minced
½ cup chunky or creamy peanut butter
3 tablespoons packed brown sugar
2 tablespoons fish sauce
1 teaspoon paprika
¼ teaspoon ground red pepper
1 cup unsweetened coconut milk
1 tablespoon water
1 tablespoon cornstarch
2 tablespoons lime juice

1. Heat oil in medium saucepan over medium-high heat. Add onion and garlic; cook and stir 2 to 3 minutes or until tender.

2. Reduce heat to medium. Add peanut butter, brown sugar, fish sauce, paprika and red pepper; stir until smooth. Slowly stir in coconut milk until well blended. (At this point, sauce may be cooled, covered and refrigerated up to 2 days in advance.)

3. Stir sauce constantly over medium heat until bubbling gently. Reduce heat to medium-low. Combine water and cornstarch in small cup; stir into sauce. Cook and stir 1 to 2 minutes or until sauce is thickened. Stir in lime juice.

Makes about 2 cups

Sesame Pork with Thai Cucumber Salad

1¼ pounds pork tenderloin
¼ cup soy sauce
2 cloves garlic, minced
    Thai Cucumber Salad (recipe follows)
3 tablespoons honey
2 tablespoons packed brown sugar
1 teaspoon minced fresh ginger
1 to 2 tablespoons toasted sesame seeds*

*To toast sesame seeds, spread seeds in small skillet. Shake skillet over medium heat about 1 minute until seeds begin to pop and turn golden.

1. Place pork in large resealable food storage bag. Combine soy sauce and garlic in small cup; pour over pork. Close bag securely; turn to coat. Marinate in refrigerator up to 2 hours. Meanwhile, prepare Thai Cucumber Salad.

2. Preheat oven to 400°F. Drain pork; reserve 1 tablespoon marinade. Combine honey, brown sugar, ginger and reserved marinade in small bowl.

3. Place pork in shallow foil-lined roasting pan. Brush with half of honey mixture. Roast 10 minutes. Turn pork over; brush with remaining honey mixture; sprinkle with sesame seeds. Roast 10 to 15 minutes or until internal temperature reaches 155°F when tested with meat thermometer inserted into thickest part.

4. Let pork stand, tented with foil, 5 minutes. (Temperature of pork will rise to 160°F.) Serve with Thai Cucumber Salad.   *Makes 4 servings*

Thai Cucumber Salad: Thinly slice 1 seedless cucumber and ½ red onion; combine in medium bowl. Combine ¼ cup rice vinegar, 2 tablespoons lime juice and 1 teaspoon sugar in small bowl; stir into cucumber mixture. Cover; refrigerate 30 minutes. Stir in 2 tablespoons chopped fresh cilantro and 2 tablespoons chopped unsalted peanuts before serving. Makes 4 servings.

Satay Beef

5 tablespoons water, divided

3½ teaspoons soy sauce, divided

2 teaspoons dark sesame oil

1 teaspoon cornstarch

1 pound beef tenderloin, cut into thin slices

2 tablespoons vegetable oil

1 medium yellow onion, coarsely chopped

1 clove garlic, minced

1 tablespoon dry sherry

1 tablespoon prepared satay sauce

1 teaspoon curry powder

½ teaspoon sugar

1. Stir 3 tablespoons water, 1½ teaspoons soy sauce and sesame oil into cornstarch in medium bowl; mix well. Add beef; stir to coat. Let stand 20 minutes.

2. Heat vegetable oil in wok or large skillet over high heat. Cook beef in batches 2 to 3 minutes or until lightly browned. Remove from wok.

3. Add onion and garlic to wok; stir-fry 3 minutes or until tender. Combine remaining 2 tablespoons water, 2 teaspoons soy sauce, sherry, satay sauce, curry powder and sugar in small cup; add to wok. When liquid boils, return meat to wok; cook and stir until thickened.   Makes 4 servings

Thai Chicken with Basil

1 small bunch fresh basil, divided
2 cups vegetable oil
6 large shallots, coarsely chopped
5 cloves garlic, minced
1 piece fresh ginger (about 1 inch square), cut into thin strips
1 pound ground chicken or turkey
2 fresh Thai chili peppers or jalapeño peppers,* cut into thin slices
2 teaspoons packed brown sugar
½ teaspoon salt
Boston lettuce leaves

*Thai chilies and jalapeño peppers can sting and irritate the skin, so wear rubber gloves when handling peppers and do not touch your eyes.

1. Set aside 8 small basil sprigs. Slice remaining basil into strips; set aside.

2. Heat oil in wok over medium-high heat until oil registers 375°F on deep-fry thermometer. Add 1 or 2 basil sprigs and deep-fry about 15 seconds or until basil is glossy and crisp. Remove with slotted spoon to paper towels; drain. Repeat with remaining sprigs, reheating oil between batches. Reserve fried basil.

3. Let oil cool slightly. Pour off most of oil leaving ¼ cup in wok. Heat over medium-high heat 30 seconds. Add shallots, garlic and ginger; cook and stir 1 minute. Add chicken and stir-fry about 4 minutes or until lightly browned. Push chicken up side of wok, letting juices remain in bottom.

4. Continue to cook about 5 to 7 minutes or until all liquid evaporates. Stir in chili slices, brown sugar and salt; cook 1 minute. Stir in reserved basil strips. Remove from heat.

5. Line serving plate with lettuce. Spoon chicken mixture on top. Top with reserved fried basil. *Makes 4 servings*

From the Sea

Thai Shrimp Curry

1 can (about 14 ounces) unsweetened coconut milk, divided
1 teaspoon Thai red curry paste
⅓ cup water
1 tablespoon packed brown sugar
1 tablespoon fish sauce
   Grated peel of 1 lime
1 pound large raw shrimp, peeled and deveined
½ cup fresh basil leaves, thinly sliced
   Hot cooked jasmine rice
   Fresh pineapple wedges (optional)
½ cup unsalted peanuts (optional)

1. Pour half of coconut milk into large skillet. Bring to a boil over medium heat, stirring occasionally. Cook 5 to 6 minutes; oil may start to rise to surface. Stir in curry paste. Cook and stir 2 minutes.

2. Stir together remaining coconut milk and water. Add to skillet with brown sugar, fish sauce and lime peel. Cook over medium-low heat 10 to 15 minutes or until sauce thickens slightly.

3. Add shrimp and basil; reduce heat to low. Cook 3 to 5 minutes or until shrimp turn pink and opaque. Serve over jasmine rice; garnish with pineapple and peanuts.   Makes 4 servings

Stir-Fried Catfish with Cucumber Rice

1 seedless cucumber

1¼ cups water

½ cup uncooked rice

4 green onions, thinly sliced

½ teaspoon white pepper

2 teaspoons canola oil

1 pound catfish fillets, cut into 1-inch chunks

1 teaspoon minced fresh ginger

1 clove garlic, minced

¼ teaspoon dark sesame oil

2 packages (6 ounces each) snow peas

1 red bell pepper, diced

¼ cup white wine or water

1 tablespoon cornstarch

1. Grate cucumber on medium side of grater into colander set over bowl; drain.

2. Combine water, rice, cucumber, green onions and white pepper in medium saucepan. Bring to a boil over medium heat. Cover; reduce heat to low. Cook about 20 minutes or until rice is tender and liquid is absorbed.

3. Heat canola oil in 12-inch nonstick skillet over high heat. Add catfish, ginger, garlic and sesame oil. Stir-fry 4 to 5 minutes or until catfish is just cooked. Add snow peas and bell pepper. Cover and cook 4 minutes.

4. Meanwhile, stir wine into cornstarch in small bowl. Pour mixture over catfish mixture; cook and stir about 2 minutes or until sauce thickens. Serve over rice. *Makes 4 servings*

Serving Suggestion: Serve with Egg Drop Soup made by stirring beaten egg into simmering reduced-sodium chicken broth seasoned with your favorite fresh chopped herbs, such as cilantro. Complete the meal with chilled fresh seasonal fruit cups or a scoop of lemon sorbet.

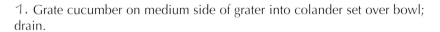

Stir-Fried Catfish with Cucumber Rice

Steamed Fish over Fragrant Thai Noodles

- **1 pound thin rice noodles or angel hair pasta**
- **4 cups chopped broccoli**
- **2 cups assorted sliced mushrooms**
- **2 cups julienned carrots**
- **1½ cups bean sprouts**
- **1 pound sole fillets**
- **¾ cup unseasoned rice vinegar**
- **½ cup reduced-sodium soy sauce**
- **2 tablespoons minced fresh ginger**
- **1 clove garlic, minced**
- **¼ cup peanut butter**
- **¾ cup thinly sliced green onions**
- **½ cup finely chopped dry-roasted peanuts**
- **¾ cup minced cilantro (optional)**

Bring 3 quarts water to a boil over high heat. Add the noodles and cook until al dente, about 3 minutes. Drain the noodles and set aside. In a wok or skillet coated with cooking spray, stir-fry the broccoli, mushrooms, carrots, and bean sprouts until softened. Toss the noodles and vegetables and set aside. Steam the sole fillets by placing the fillets on a glass plate. Cover with plastic wrap or a glass lid. Microwave on high for 3 to 4 minutes. (Or bake the fillets wrapped in foil in a 450°F oven for 4 to 6 minutes.)

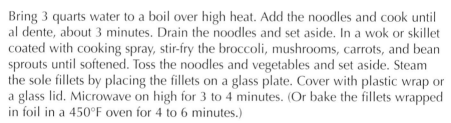

To make the dressing, combine the rice vinegar, soy sauce, ginger and garlic in a small bowl. Microwave the peanut butter on high until it reaches a liquid like consistency. Whisk the peanut butter into the dressing. Pour the dressing over the noodles and vegetables and toss well. Arrange the steamed fish fillets on top. Garnish with green onions, peanuts and cilantro.

Makes 6 servings

Favorite recipe from **Peanut Advisory Board**

Thai Seafood Stir-Fry

2 tablespoons lemon juice
1 tablespoon cornstarch
1 tablespoon soy sauce
2 teaspoons sugar
½ teaspoon ground ginger
¼ teaspoon red pepper flakes
8 ounces broccoli
2 stalks celery
3 tablespoons vegetable oil
1 large onion, sliced
¼ cup water
1 pound imitation crabmeat
½ cup sliced water chestnuts
3 cups hot cooked rice

1. Combine lemon juice, cornstarch, soy sauce, sugar, ginger and red pepper flakes in small bowl; stir until smooth. Set aside.

2. Cut broccoli into small florets. Cut celery diagonally into ½-inch slices.

3. Heat oil in wok or large skillet over high heat 1 minute. Add onion; stir-fry 1 minute. Add broccoli and celery; stir-fry 2 minutes. Reduce heat to medium-high. Add water; cover and cook until vegetables are crisp-tender. Add crabmeat and water chestnuts; stir-fry 1 minute.

4. Stir cornstarch mixture; add to wok. Stir-fry until sauce boils and thickens. Serve with rice.   *Makes 6 servings*

Note: Imitation crabmeat is processed fish, typically pollack, that is flavored and restructured to make seafood products. It comes in flakes, chunks, sticks or nuggets and is flavored like crabmeat or lobster.

Thai Seafood Kabobs with Spicy Peanut Rice

1¼ cups UNCLE BEN'S® ORIGINAL CONVERTED® Brand Rice
1 pound medium raw shrimp, peeled and deveined, with tails intact
½ pound bay scallops
¼ cup soy sauce
2 tablespoons sesame oil
1 large red bell pepper, cut into 1-inch squares
6 green onions with tops, cut into 1-inch pieces
½ cup prepared Thai peanut sauce*
½ cup chopped peanuts

*Thai peanut sauce can be found in the Asian section of large supermarket

1. Cook rice according to package directions.

2. Meanwhile, place shrimp and scallops in medium bowl. Combine soy sauce and sesame oil; pour half of mixture over shellfish, tossing to coat. Let stand 15 minutes. Reserve remaining soy sauce mixture for basting.

3. Alternately thread shrimp, scallops, bell pepper and green onions onto twelve 12-inch metal skewers. Brush with half the reserved soy sauce mixture. Spoon Thai peanut sauce over each skewer, coating evenly. Grill or broil 8 minutes or until shrimp are pink and scallops are opaque, turning and brushing once with remaining soy sauce mixture and Thai peanut sauce.

4. Stir peanuts into cooked rice; place on serving platter. Top with seafood kabobs. Serve immediately.   *Makes 6 servings*

Serving Suggestion: Garnish with minced fresh cilantro, if desired.

Thai Seafood Kabobs with Spicy Peanut Rice

Spicy Thai Shrimp Soup

1 tablespoon vegetable oil
1 pound medium raw shrimp, peeled and deveined, shells reserved
1 jalapeño pepper,* cut into slivers
1 tablespoon paprika
$\frac{1}{4}$ teaspoon ground red pepper
4 cans (about 14 ounces each) reduced-sodium chicken broth
  $\frac{1}{2}$-inch strip *each* lemon and lime peel
1 can (15 ounces) straw mushrooms, drained
  Juice of 1 lemon
  Juice of 1 lime
2 tablespoons soy sauce
1 Thai chili pepper or jalapeño pepper, cut into strips*
$\frac{1}{4}$ cup chopped fresh cilantro

Jalapeño and Thai chili peppers can sting and irritate the skin, so wear rubber gloves when handling peppers and do not touch your eyes.

1. Heat oil in wok or large skillet over medium-high heat 1 minute. Add shrimp and jalapeño pepper slivers; stir-fry 1 minute. Add paprika and ground red pepper. Stir-fry 1 minute more or until shrimp turn pink and opaque. Remove shrimp mixture to bowl; set aside.

2. Add shrimp shells to wok and stir-fry 30 seconds. Add chicken broth and lemon and lime peels; bring to a boil. Cover; reduce heat to low. Simmer 15 minutes.

3. Remove shells and peels from broth with slotted spoon; discard. Add mushrooms and shrimp mixture to broth; bring to a boil. Stir in lemon and lime juices, soy sauce and Thai chili pepper. Ladle soup into bowls. Sprinkle with cilantro. Serve immediately.   *Makes 8 first-course servings*

Scallops, Shrimp and Squid with Basil and Chilies

8 ounces cleaned squid (body tubes, tentacles, or a combination)
8 ounces scallops
1/4 cup water
2 tablespoons oyster sauce
1 teaspoon cornstarch
8 to 12 ounces medium raw shrimp, peeled
1 tablespoon vegetable oil
4 jalapeño peppers,* seeded and thinly sliced
6 cloves garlic, minced
1/2 cup roasted peanuts, salted or unsalted
2 green onions, thinly sliced
1/2 cup slivered fresh basil leaves
   Hot cooked rice

Jalapeño peppers can sting and irritate the skin, so wear rubber gloves when handling peppers and do not touch your eyes.

1. Rinse squid; cut body tubes crosswise into 1/3-inch rings. Rinse and drain scallops. Slice large scallops crosswise into halves. Combine water, oyster sauce and cornstarch in small bowl; set aside.

2. Bring 4 cups water to a boil in medium saucepan over high heat. Add shrimp; reduce heat to medium. Cook 2 to 3 minutes or until shrimp turn pink and opaque. Remove with slotted spoon to colander.

3. Return water to a boil. Add squid; reduce heat to medium. Cook rings 1 minute; cook tentacles 4 minutes. Remove to colander. Return water to a boil. Add scallops; reduce heat to medium. Cook 3 to 4 minutes or until opaque. Remove to colander.

4. Heat oil in wok over medium-high heat. Add jalapeño peppers; cook and stir 3 minutes. Add garlic; cook and stir 2 minutes or until peppers are tender.

5. Stir cornstarch mixture; add to wok. Cook and stir until thickened. Add seafood, peanuts and green onions; cook and stir 2 to 3 minutes or until heated through. Stir in basil. Serve with rice.   *Makes 4 servings*

Curried Shrimp with Coconut Ginger Rice

Coconut Ginger Rice (recipe follows)
1 tablespoon vegetable oil
1 pound medium raw shrimp, peeled and deveined
3 cloves garlic, minced
1 cup finely chopped fresh pineapple *or* 1 can (8 ounces) crushed pineapple, drained
2 tablespoons packed brown sugar
1 tablespoon fish sauce
2 teaspoons curry powder
¼ teaspoon red pepper flakes
3 green onions, thinly sliced
Toasted coconut, chopped peanuts, diced red bell pepper and chopped fresh cilantro (optional)

1. Prepare Coconut Ginger Rice. Meanwhile, heat oil in large skillet over high heat. Add shrimp and garlic; cook and stir 2 to 3 minutes, until shrimp turn pink and opaque. Transfer to bowl with slotted spoon.

2. Add pineapple, brown sugar, fish sauce, curry powder and red pepper flakes to skillet; bring to a boil, stirring constantly. Reduce heat to medium; cook 2 minutes. Stir in shrimp mixture and green onions; cook 1 minute or until shrimp are heated through.

5. Serve with Coconut Ginger Rice, toasted coconut, peanuts, red bell pepper and cilantro. *Makes 4 servings*

Coconut Ginger Rice: Bring 3 cups water, 2 cups rice, 1 cup unsweetened coconut milk, 2 tablespoons sugar and 2 teaspoons grated fresh ginger to a boil in large saucepan over high heat. Reduce heat to low; cover and simmer 25 minutes or until liquid is absorbed. Fluff rice with fork. Makes about 6 cups.

Curried Shrimp with
Coconut Ginger Rice

Spicy Thai Warm Shrimp Salad

¾ cup prepared vinaigrette salad dressing

⅓ cup chopped fresh mint leaves

¼ cup *Frank's® RedHot®* XTRA Hot Sauce or *Frank's® RedHot®* Cayenne
  Pepper Sauce

¼ cup *French's®* Honey Dijon Mustard

1 tablespoon lime juice

1 tablespoon sucralose sugar substitute

1 tablespoon vegetable oil

1½ pounds large shrimp, shelled with tails left on

8 cups shredded Napa cabbage

1 red bell pepper, thinly sliced

1 cup thinly sliced cucumber

1. Combine salad dressing, mint, XTRA Hot Sauce, mustard, lime juice and sugar substitute in large bowl; set aside.

2. Heat oil in large nonstick skillet or wok until hot. Stir-fry shrimp 2 to 3 minutes until shrimp turn pink. Transfer to bowl with dressing. Add cabbage, bell pepper and cucumber; toss to coat. Serve warm.

Makes 6 servings

Prep Time: 10 minutes
Cook Time: 5 minutes

Spicy Thai Warm Shrimp Salad

Baked Fish with Thai Pesto

1 to 2 jalapeño peppers,* coarsely chopped
1 lemon
4 green onions, thinly sliced
2 tablespoons chopped fresh ginger
3 cloves garlic, minced
1½ cups lightly packed fresh basil leaves
1 cup lightly packed fresh cilantro leaves
¼ cup lightly packed fresh mint leaves
¼ cup roasted peanuts
2 tablespoons sweetened shredded coconut
½ teaspoon sugar
½ cup peanut oil
2 pounds boneless fish fillets (such as salmon, halibut, cod or orange roughy)
Lemon and cucumber slices (optional)

Jalapeño peppers can sting and irritate the skin, so wear rubber gloves when handling peppers and do not touch your eyes.

1. Place jalapeño peppers in blender or food processor.

2. Grate peel of lemon. Juice lemon to measure 2 tablespoons. Add peel and juice to blender.

3. Add green onions, ginger, garlic, basil, cilantro, mint, peanuts, coconut and sugar to blender; blend until finely chopped. With motor running, slowly pour in oil; blend until mixed.

4. Preheat oven to 375°F. Rinse fish and pat dry with paper towels. Place fillets on lightly oiled baking sheet. Spread solid thin layer of pesto over each fillet.

5. Bake 10 minutes or until fish begins to flake when tested with fork and is just opaque in center. Transfer fish to serving platter with wide spatula. Garnish with lemon and cucumber slices. *Makes 4 to 6 servings*

Thai-Style Tuna Steaks

2 tablespoons reduced-sodium soy sauce
2 teaspoons brown sugar
1 teaspoon ground cumin
1 teaspoon sesame oil or vegetable oil
¼ teaspoon crushed red pepper
1 clove garlic, minced
4 (4- to 5-ounce) tuna steaks
4 green onions, diagonally sliced
3 cups cooked white rice

Combine soy sauce, brown sugar, cumin, sesame oil, red pepper and garlic in a 11×7-inch microwave-safe baking dish. Add tuna and turn to coat both sides. Let marinate 5 to 15 minutes.

Turn tuna over and cover with lid or waxed paper. Microwave at HIGH (100% power) 1½ minutes, rotating dish ¼ turn. Sprinkle with green onions and continue to cook 1½ minutes longer or until tuna begins to flake easily when tested with a fork. Let stand, covered, 2 minutes. Serve tuna and sauce over rice.

Makes 4 servings

Favorite recipe from **National Fisheries Institute**

Sesame oil comes in two basic types. Dark sesame oil, which is the kind used in most Asian cuisines, has a strong flavor and fragrance. It is sometimes called toasted sesame oil, or Asian sesame oil. The lighter sesame oil has a much milder flavor and can be used for frying and in salad dressings. Dark sesame oil is a delightful flavor accent, but should be used sparingly as it can easily become overwhelming.

Noodles & Rice

Vegetarian Asian Noodles with Peanut Sauce

½ **package (about 9 ounces) uncooked udon noodles*** *or*
    4 ounces uncooked whole wheat spaghetti

1 **tablespoon vegetable oil**

2 **cups fresh snow peas, sliced diagonally**

1 **cup shredded carrots**

¼ **cup hot water**

¼ **cup peanut butter**

¼ **cup chopped green onions**

2 **to 4 tablespoons chili garlic sauce**

1 **tablespoon soy sauce**

¼ **cup dry-roasted peanuts**

*Udon noodles, wheat flour noodles, are usually available in the Asian section of natural food stores or larger supermarkets.

1. Cook noodles according to package directions. Drain, set aside.

2. Heat oil in large skillet over medium-high heat. Add carrots and snow peas; cook 2 minutes. Remove from heat.

3. Add water, peanut butter, green onions, chili sauce and soy sauce; mix well. Stir in noodles; toss well to coat. Sprinkle with peanuts. Serve warm or at room temperature.

Makes 4 servings

Rice Noodles with Broccoli and Tofu

1 package (14 ounces) firm or extra firm tofu

1 package (8 to 10 ounces) wide rice noodles

2 tablespoons peanut oil

3 medium shallots, sliced

6 cloves garlic, minced

1 jalapeño pepper,* minced

2 teaspoons minced fresh ginger

3 cups broccoli florets

3 tablespoons regular soy sauce

1 tablespoon sweet soy sauce (or substitute regular)

1 to 2 tablespoons fish sauce

Fresh basil leaves (optional)

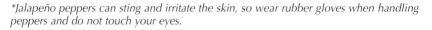

Jalapeño peppers can sting and irritate the skin, so wear rubber gloves when handling peppers and do not touch your eyes.

1. Slice tofu horizontally into 2 pieces. Place tofu on cutting board between layers of paper towels; put another cutting board on top and add a weight to press moisture out of tofu. Soak rice noodles in large bowl filled with warm water; let stand 30 minutes or until soft.

2. Meanwhile, heat oil in large skillet or wok. Cut tofu into bite-sized squares and blot dry. Stir-fry about 5 minutes or until tofu is speckled and light brown on all sides. Remove and reserve.

3. Add shallots, garlic, jalapeño pepper and ginger to skillet. Stir-fry over medium-high heat 2 to 3 minutes; add broccoli and stir-fry. Cover; cook 3 minutes or until broccoli is crisp-tender.

4. Drain noodles well, add to skillet and stir to combine. Return tofu to skillet; add soy sauces and fish sauce; stir-fry about 8 minutes or until noodles are coated and flavors are blended. Garnish with basil.

Makes 4 to 6 servings

Cellophane Noodle Salad

1 package (about 4 ounces) cellophane* noodles

2 tablespoons peanut or vegetable oil

8 ounces medium or large raw shrimp, peeled and deveined

3 cloves garlic, minced

¼ teaspoon red pepper flakes

½ cup cooked pork or ham strips (optional)

2 tablespoons soy sauce

1 tablespoon fresh lemon juice

1 tablespoon rice vinegar

1 tablespoon dark sesame oil

⅓ cup thinly sliced green onions or coarsely chopped fresh cilantro

Cellophane noodles are available in the Asian section of most supermarkets. They are also called bean thread or glass noodles.

1. Place cellophane noodles in medium bowl; cover with warm water. Soak 15 minutes to soften. Drain well; cut into 2-inch pieces.

2. Meanwhile, heat peanut oil in wok or large skillet over medium-high heat. Add shrimp, garlic and red pepper flakes; stir-fry 2 minutes. Add pork, if desired, soy sauce, lemon juice, vinegar and sesame oil; stir-fry 1 minute.

3. Add cellophane noodles; stir-fry 1 minute or until heated through. Serve warm, chilled or at room temperature. Sprinkle with green onions before serving.   *Makes 4 servings*

Cellophane Noodle Salad

Thai Meatballs and Noodles

Thai Meatballs (recipe follows)
12 ounces uncooked egg noodles
2 cans (about 14 ounces each) reduced-sodium chicken broth
2 tablespoons packed brown sugar
2 tablespoons fish sauce or soy sauce
1 small piece fresh ginger (about 1×½ inch), cut into thin strips
1 medium carrot, cut into matchstick-size strips
1 pound bok choy, cut into ½-inch-wide strips
½ cup slivered fresh mint or basil leaves

1. Prepare Thai Meatballs. While meatballs are cooking, cook noodles according to package directions; drain. Transfer noodles to large serving bowl; keep warm.

2. Heat chicken broth in large saucepan or wok over high heat. Add brown sugar, fish sauce and ginger; stir until sugar is dissolved. Add meatballs and carrot to saucepan; bring to a boil. Reduce heat to medium-low; cover and simmer 15 minutes or until meatballs are heated through.

3. Add bok choy; simmer 4 to 5 minutes or until stalks are crisp-tender. Stir in mint; spoon mixture over noodles in serving bowl.   *Makes 6 servings*

Thai Meatballs

1½ pounds ground beef or pork
¼ cup chopped fresh basil
¼ cup chopped fresh mint
2 tablespoons minced fresh ginger
1 tablespoon fish sauce
6 cloves garlic, minced
1 teaspoon ground cinnamon
½ teaspoon whole fennel seeds, crushed
½ teaspoon black pepper
2 tablespoons peanut oil, divided

1. Combine beef, basil, mint, ginger, fish sauce, garlic, cinnamon, fennel and pepper in large bowl; mix until well blended. Rub cutting board with 1 tablespoon oil. Pat meat mixture into 12×8-inch rectangle on board. Cut into 32 squares. Shape each square into a ball.

2. Heat remaining 1 tablespoon oil in large skillet or wok over medium-high heat. Add meatballs in single layer; cook 8 to 10 minutes or until no longer pink in center, turning to brown all sides. (Cook in several batches.) Remove meatballs with slotted spoon to paper towels; drain.

Makes 32 meatballs

Spicy Thai Rice

2 cups water
1 cup uncooked long grain white rice
¼ cup chopped green onions
2 fresh red chiles, seeded and chopped
1 tablespoon snipped cilantro
1 tablespoon margarine
1 teaspoon minced fresh gingerroot
¾ teaspoon salt
⅛ teaspoon ground turmeric
1 to 2 teaspoons lime juice
   Chopped roasted peanuts for garnish (optional)
   Red pepper flakes for garnish (optional)

Combine water, rice, onions, chiles, cilantro, margarine, gingerroot, salt and turmeric in 2- to 3-quart saucepan. Bring to a boil; stir once or twice. Reduce heat; cover and simmer 15 minutes or until rice is tender and liquid is absorbed. Stir in lime juice; fluff with fork. Garnish with peanuts and red pepper flakes.

Makes 6 servings

Favorite recipe from **USA Rice**

Lemon-Ginger Chicken with Puffed Rice Noodles

Vegetable oil for frying
4 ounces rice noodles, broken in half
3 boneless skinless chicken breasts, cut into 2½×1-inch strips
1 stalk lemongrass, cut into 1-inch pieces
3 cloves garlic, minced
1 teaspoon minced fresh ginger
¼ teaspoon *each* ground red pepper and black pepper
¼ cup water
1 tablespoon cornstarch
2 tablespoons peanut oil
6 ounces fresh snow peas, ends trimmed
1 can (8¾ ounces) baby corn, rinsed and drained
¼ cup chopped fresh cilantro
2 tablespoons packed brown sugar
2 tablespoons fish sauce
1 tablespoon soy sauce

1. Heat 3 inches vegetable oil in wok or Dutch oven until oil registers 375°F on deep-fry thermometer. Fry noodles in small batches 20 seconds or until puffy, holding down noodles in oil with slotted spoon to fry evenly. Drain on paper towels; set aside.

2. Combine chicken, lemongrass, garlic, ginger, red pepper and black pepper in medium bowl. Stir water into cornstarch in small bowl; set aside.

3. Heat peanut oil in wok over high heat 1 minute. Add chicken mixture; stir-fry 3 minutes or until cooked through.

4. Add snow peas and baby corn; stir-fry 1 to 2 minutes. Stir cornstarch mixture; add to wok. Cook 1 minute or until thickened.

5. Add cilantro, brown sugar, fish sauce and soy sauce; cook until heated through. Discard lemongrass. Serve over rice noodles.

Makes 4 servings

Lemon-Ginger Chicken with Puffed Rice Noodles

Pad Thai

8 ounces uncooked rice noodles

2 tablespoons rice vinegar

1½ tablespoons fish sauce

1 to 2 tablespoons lemon juice

1 tablespoon ketchup

2 teaspoons sugar

¼ teaspoon red pepper flakes

1 tablespoon vegetable oil

1 boneless skinless chicken breast (about 4 ounces), finely chopped

2 green onions, thinly sliced

2 cloves garlic, minced

3 ounces small raw shrimp, peeled

2 cups bean sprouts

¾ cup shredded red cabbage

1 medium carrot, shredded

3 tablespoons minced fresh cilantro

2 tablespoons chopped unsalted dry-roasted peanuts

Lime wedges

1. Place noodles in medium bowl. Cover with warm water; let stand 30 minutes or until soft. Drain and set aside. Combine vinegar, fish sauce, lemon juice, ketchup, sugar and red pepper flakes in small bowl.

2. Heat oil in wok or large nonstick skillet over medium-high heat. Add chicken, green onions and garlic. Cook and stir until chicken is cooked through. Stir in noodles; cook 1 minute. Add shrimp; cook 3 minutes or until shrimp turn pink and opaque. Stir in fish sauce mixture; toss to coat evenly. Add bean sprouts and cook until heated through, about 2 minutes.

3. Serve with shredded cabbage, carrot, cilantro, peanuts and lime wedges.

Makes 5 servings

Thai Curry Stir-Fry

½ cup reduced-sodium chicken broth

2 teaspoons cornstarch

2 teaspoons soy sauce

1½ teaspoons curry powder

⅛ teaspoon red pepper flakes

Olive oil cooking spray

3 green onions, sliced

2 cloves garlic, minced

2 cups broccoli florets

⅔ cup sliced carrot

1½ teaspoons olive oil

6 ounces boneless skinless chicken breasts, cut into bite-size pieces

⅔ cup hot cooked rice

1. Stir together broth, cornstarch, soy sauce, curry powder and red pepper flakes in small bowl. Set aside.

2. Spray nonstick wok or large nonstick skillet with cooking spray. Heat over medium-high heat. Add green onions and garlic; stir-fry 1 minute. Remove from wok.

3. Add broccoli and carrot to wok; stir-fry 2 to 3 minutes or until crisp-tender. Remove from wok.

4. Add oil to hot wok. Add chicken and stir-fry 2 to 3 minutes or until cooked through. Stir broth mixture; add to wok. Cook and stir until broth mixture comes to a boil and thickens slightly. Return all vegetables to wok. Heat through. Serve over rice.

Makes 2 servings

Thai Fried Rice

2½ cups water

1⅓ cups jasmine or long-grain white rice

8 ounces ground pork or pork sausage

1 tablespoon vegetable oil

1 medium onion, thinly sliced

1 tablespoon minced fresh ginger

1 jalapeño pepper,* seeded and finely chopped

3 cloves garlic, minced

½ teaspoon ground turmeric or paprika

2 tablespoons fish sauce

2 cups chopped cooked vegetables such as broccoli, zucchini, red bell peppers, carrots, bok choy or spinach

3 eggs, lightly beaten

3 green onions, thinly sliced

½ cup chopped fresh cilantro

Jalapeños can sting and irritate the skin, so wear rubber gloves when handling peppers and do not touch your eyes.

1. Bring water and rice to a boil in medium saucepan over high heat. Reduce heat to low; cover and simmer 20 minutes or until water is absorbed.

2. Fluff rice with fork. Let cool to room temperature. Cover and refrigerate until cold, at least 1 hour or up to 24 hours.

3. When rice is cold, cook pork in wok or large skillet over medium-high heat until no longer pink. Drain off excess fat; transfer pork to bowl and set aside.

4. Heat oil in wok over medium-high heat. Add onion, ginger, jalapeño pepper, garlic and turmeric; stir-fry 4 to 6 minutes or until onion is tender.

5. Stir in fish sauce; mix well. Stir in cold rice, vegetables and pork; cook and stir 3 to 4 minutes or until heated through.

6. Push rice mixture up sides of wok and pour eggs into center. Cook eggs 2 to 3 minutes or just until set, lifting and stirring to scramble. Stir rice mixture into eggs.

7. Stir in green onions. Transfer to serving bowl; sprinkle with cilantro.

Makes 4 servings

Thailand Peanut Pesto

1 cup unsalted roasted peanuts

$\frac{1}{2}$ cup soy sauce

$\frac{1}{2}$ cup sesame oil

1 teaspoon TABASCO® brand Pepper Sauce

$\frac{1}{4}$ cup honey

$\frac{1}{3}$ cup water

3 cloves garlic, minced

12 ounces bow tie pasta, cooked according to package directions, drained
  Chopped green onions for garnish

Place peanuts in food processor; process until finely ground. With motor running, add soy sauce, sesame oil, TABASCO® Sauce, honey, water and garlic cloves one at a time, through feed tube. Process until a thick, smooth paste has formed. Transfer mixture to bowl; refrigerate, covered, until ready to use. Toss with bow tie pasta and garnish with chopped green onions.

Makes 4 servings

Thai-Style Warm Noodle Salad

8 ounces uncooked angel hair pasta
$\frac{1}{2}$ cup chunky peanut butter
$\frac{1}{4}$ cup soy sauce
$\frac{1}{4}$ to $\frac{1}{2}$ teaspoon red pepper flakes
2 green onions, thinly sliced
1 carrot, shredded

1. Cook pasta according to package directions.

2. Meanwhile, blend peanut butter, soy sauce and red pepper flakes in serving bowl until smooth.

3. Drain pasta, reserving 5 tablespoons water. Mix hot pasta water with peanut butter mixture until smooth; toss pasta with sauce. Stir in green onions and carrot. Serve warm or at room temperature.   *Makes 4 servings*

Notes: This salad is as versatile as it is easy to make. It can be prepared a day ahead and served warm or cold—perfect for potlucks, picnics and even lunch boxes. You can also make it into a heartier meal by mixing in any leftover chicken or beef.

Prep and Cook Time: 12 minutes

Thai-Style Warm Noodle Salad

Chicken Thai Stir-Fry

4 boneless, skinless chicken breast halves, cut into ½-inch strips
2 tablespoons vegetable oil
2 teaspoons grated fresh ginger
2 cloves garlic, minced
2 cups broccoli flowerets
1 medium yellow squash, cut into ¼-inch slices
1 medium red bell pepper, cut into 2-inch strips
⅓ cup creamy peanut butter
¼ cup reduced-sodium soy sauce
2 tablespoons white vinegar
2 teaspoons brown sugar
½ teaspoon crushed red pepper
⅓ cup reduced-sodium chicken broth, fat skimmed
8 ounces linguine, cooked according to package directions
2 green onions, white and green parts, thinly sliced

In large skillet, heat oil over medium-high heat. Add chicken, ginger and garlic; cook and stir about 5 minutes or until chicken is lightly browned and fork-tender. Remove chicken mixture to bowl; set aside. To drippings in same skillet, add broccoli, squash and red bell pepper strips. Cook, stirring, about 5 minutes or until vegetables are crisp-tender. Remove vegetables to bowl with chicken; set aside. To same skillet, add peanut butter, soy sauce, vinegar, brown sugar and crushed red pepper; stir in chicken broth. Return chicken and vegetables to pan; heat through. Serve over linguine. Sprinkle with green onions. *Makes 4 servings*

*Favorite recipe from **Delmarva Poultry Industry, Inc.***

Contents

Japanese cuisine is known for using the highest quality seasonal ingredients and presenting them beautifully. Tempura, teriyaki and especially sushi have become mainstream favorites in restaurants across the country. Creating the distinctive flavors and unique look of Japanese food in a home kitchen is less difficult than you would think and can also be a wonderful excuse for getting together with friends. Try having a sushi rolling party or break out the chopsticks and treat friends to a simple teriyaki dinner. The recipes in this book are written with techniques and ingredients that will be mostly familiar to you. A few less mainstream products, such as miso or nori, can usually be found in the Asian aisle of a supermarket or purchased on-line.

Doing the Dip

Many classic Japanese preparations include at least one dipping sauce. It can be nothing more than soy sauce with optional wasabi as it is for sushi, or something more elaborate, such as a ponzu sauce for Teppankayi (page 232). These sauces are an important part of the final seasoning and are served in small individual dishes. You may wish to purchase special dishes if you serve Asian food often, or simply use small custard cups or bowls

Knowing Your Beans

The soybean is used in many forms in Japanese cooking. Soy sauce (called shoyu) is a frequent ingredient, as is the Japanese variation, tamari. While tamari and soy sauce are close enough in flavor to be substituted for each other, tamari is a bit more robust.

Tofu or bean curd is an important source of protein, especially for vegetarians. It is grilled, fried, stir-fried, mashed and even made into ice cream. When purchasing tofu, check expiration dates. Some brands are refrigerated, others are sold in shelf-stable boxes. Most brands offer a choice of textures—soft, firm or extra firm. Silken tofu is so called because it has an extremely smooth texture. It is also less sturdy and harder to handle in any recipe that requires the tofu to keep its shape. After opening, all tofu should be refrigerated, covered with fresh water daily, and used within a week.

Sushi Made Simple

A Japanese sushi chef spends years perfecting his craft and the raw fish served is of a quality that is unavailable to home cooks, but that doesn't mean you shouldn't try sushi at home. The recipes in this book will let you enjoy the experience without the stress. No need for raw fish or fancy knives. You can even come up with your own filling ideas—anything from tuna salad to leftover tempura is fair game. It may take you a try or two to get the hang of rolling nori around a filling, but even the mistakes are delicious!

pg. 208   pg. 234   pg. 248

Glossary

dashi: Used in miso soup and many other Japanese recipes, dashi is a stock or broth made with dried bonito (tuna) flakes and kelp.

ginger, pickled: These thin slices of fresh ginger are preserved in a vinegar pickling solution and served with sushi or used as a garnish.

mirin: Mirin is a very sweet golden wine used in many sauces, marinades and glazes. It is not usually consumed as a beverage.

miso: This salty paste made of fermented soybeans, rice and/or barley comes in many varieties, but white miso (actually yellow in color) is the mildest and easiest to find.

nori: These paper-thin sheets of seaweed are dry and dark greenish black. Most nori is used to wrap sushi and is pre-toasted (yaki-nori).

panko bread crumbs: This Japanese-style bread crumb gives a lighter, crisper texture to fried foods. Panko is coarser and flakier than ordinary bread crumbs.

ponzu sauce: A Japanese citrus called yuzu is used to make this classic soy-based dipping sauce. The flavor can be approximated by substituting lemon and orange juice. (See the recipe for Teppanyaki on page 232 for a version.)

sake: A slightly sweet rice wine, sake is drunk warm or chilled and also used in cooking. While it is brewed from rice, as is mirin, it is less sweet and has a different flavor.

sushi: It's not just raw fish! Sushi is always made from rice flavored with sweetened rice vinegar. It can be topped or rolled with fish, vegetables and pickles and is served in bite-size pieces.

sushi rice: Rice prepared for sushi is the short grain variety, cooked, then quickly cooled and dressed with sweetened vinegar which gives it a glossy sheen.

tamari: A Japanese sauce similar to soy, Tamari has a slightly thicker consistency and a stronger but mellower flavor.

teriyaki sauce: This popular marinade is made from soy sauce, ginger, sake and sugar. Teriyaki sauce gives meat, poultry and tofu a salty-sweet taste and a glazed appearance.

soba noodles: Buckwheat gives these noodles their dark brown color and slightly chewy texture. They are often served cold with a dipping sauce.

udon noodles: These thick wheat noodles are similar to spaghetti. Udon noodles are served hot in the summer and cold in the winter. Toppings can include fried tofu, fish cakes or almost any meat or vegetable.

wasabi: This bright green condiment is sold in the form of a powder, which must be reconstituted with water, or as a paste. It has the same powerful, sinus-clearing flavor as horseradish. In fact, most prepared wasabi IS horseradish tinted green. The true wasabi root is rarely available, even in Japan, and costs 10 times as much as horseradish, to which it is related.

Starters and Sides

Japanese Petal Salad

1 pound medium shrimp, cooked *or* 2 cups chicken, cooked
   and shredded
   Romaine lettuce leaves
2 fresh California Nectarines, halved, pitted and thinly sliced
2 cups sliced cucumber
2 celery stalks, cut into 3-inch strips
⅓ cup shredded red radishes
   Sesame Dressing (recipe follows) or low calorie dressing
2 teaspoons sesame seeds (optional)

Center shrimp on 4 lettuce-lined salad plates. Fan nectarines to right side of shrimp; overlap cucumber slices to left side. Place celery at top of plate; mound radishes at bottom of plate. Prepare dressing; pour 3 tablespoons over each salad. Sprinkle with sesame seeds, if desired.   *Makes 4 servings*

Sesame Dressing: In small bowl, combine ½ cup rice wine vinegar (not seasoned type), 2 tablespoons reduced-sodium soy sauce, 2 teaspoons sugar and 2 teaspoons dark sesame oil. Stir until sugar is dissolved.

*Favorite recipe from **California Tree Fruit Agreement***

Spicy Sesame Noodles

6 ounces uncooked soba (buckwheat) noodles
2 teaspoons dark sesame oil
1 tablespoon sesame seeds
$\frac{1}{2}$ cup reduced-sodium chicken broth
1 tablespoon creamy peanut butter
$\frac{1}{2}$ cup thinly sliced green onions
$\frac{1}{2}$ cup minced red bell pepper
4 teaspoons soy sauce
1$\frac{1}{2}$ teaspoons finely chopped seeded jalapeño pepper*
1 clove garlic, minced
$\frac{1}{4}$ teaspoon red pepper flakes

Jalapeño peppers can sting and irritate the skin, so wear rubber gloves when handling peppers and do not touch your eyes.

1. Cook noodles according to package directions. (Do not overcook.) Rinse noodles thoroughly with cold water; drain. Place noodles in large bowl; toss with oil.

2. Place sesame seeds in small skillet. Cook over medium heat about 3 minutes or until seeds begin to pop and turn golden brown, stirring frequently. Remove from heat; set aside.

3. Combine chicken broth and peanut butter in small bowl with wire whisk until blended. (Mixture may look curdled.) Stir in green onions, bell pepper, soy sauce, jalapeño pepper, garlic and red pepper flakes.

4. Pour mixture over noodles; toss to coat. Cover and let stand 30 minutes at room temperature or refrigerate up to 24 hours. Sprinkle with toasted sesame seeds before serving. Makes 6 servings

Bite-You-Back Roasted Edamame

2 teaspoons vegetable oil

2 teaspoons honey

¼ teaspoon wasabi powder*

1 package (10 ounces) shelled edamame, thawed if frozen

Kosher salt

Available in the Asian section of most supermarkets and in Asian specialty markets.

1. Preheat oven to 375°F.

2. Stir together oil, honey and wasabi powder in large bowl. Add edamame and toss to coat. Transfer to baking sheet and arrange in single layer.

3. Bake for 12 to 15 minutes or until edamame are golden brown, stirring once. Remove from baking sheet immediately; sprinkle liberally with kosher salt.

4. Cool completely and store in airtight container until ready to serve.

Makes 4 servings

tip

Edamame are fresh green soy beans. They are usually available in the frozen section of the supermarket with or without their pods. In Japan, salted edamame in the pod are often served as a tasty bar snack. Since they are high in protein and low in fat, snacking on edamame makes good nutritional sense, too. Edamame also make excellent additions to soups, salads and casseroles. Try mixing corn with edamame, too, for a twist on succotash.

Vegetarian Sushi

1¼ cups Japanese short grain sushi rice*
1½ cups water
  1 teaspoon dark sesame oil
  4 medium shiitake mushrooms, sliced thin
 ½ red bell pepper
 ½ seedless cucumber
  4 thin asparagus spears
2½ tablespoons seasoned rice vinegar
  3 sheets nori (from .6 ounce package)
    Prepared wasabi
    Pickled ginger, soy sauce and additional prepared wasabi

If you can't find white rice labeled "sushi rice", use any short grain rice.

1. Rinse rice in several changes of water to remove excess starch; swish rice around and drain until water almost runs clear. Drain and place in medium saucepan. Cover; bring to a boil quickly. Reduce heat; cook, covered, over very low heat 15 to 20 minutes until rice is tender and liquid absorbed. Let stand 10 minutes, covered.

2. Meanwhile, prepare fillings. Heat small nonstick skillet over medium heat; add sesame oil. Cook and stir mushrooms 2 minutes or until tender. Slice bell pepper into very thin, long pieces. Cut cucumber into thin, long slivers, leaving skin on. Wrap asparagus in plastic wrap and microwave 1 minute to blanch.

3. Gently spoon warm rice into shallow nonmetallic bowl. Sprinkle vinegar over rice and fold in gently with wooden spoon trying not to crush rice grains. Cut sheet of nori in half lengthwise, parallel to lines marked on rough side. Place lengthwise, shiny side down, on bamboo rolling mat about 3 slats from edge nearest to you.

4. Prepare small bowl with water and a splash of vinegar to rinse fingers and prevent rice from sticking while working. Spread about ½ cup rice over nori, leaving ½-inch border at top edge. Spread pinch of wasabi across center of rice. Arrange strips of 2 different fillings over wasabi. Choose any 2, but do not overfill.

continued on page 204

Vegetarian Sushi, continued

5. Pick up edge of mat nearest you. Roll mat forward, wrapping rice around fillings and pressing gently to form log. Once roll is formed, press gently to seal and shape; place completed roll on cutting board, seam side down. Repeat with remaining nori and fillings.

6. Slice each roll into 6 pieces with sharp knife. Wipe knife with damp cloth between cuts. Arrange sushi on serving plates with pickled ginger, soy sauce and additional wasabi.   Makes six sushi rolls (36 pieces)

Miso Soup with Tofu

- ½ cup dried bonito flakes*
- 4 cups chicken broth
- 2 teaspoons vegetable oil
- 1 leek, white part only, finely chopped
- 1 tablespoon white miso**
- 8 ounces firm tofu, cut into ½-inch cubes (about 1½ cups)

*Dried bonito flakes (katsuobushi) are available in the Asian section of large supermarkets or in Asian stores. If unavailable, skip step one and add an additional 1 tablespoon miso.

**A fermented soybean paste used frequently in Japanese cooking. Miso comes in many varieties; the light yellow miso, usually labeled "white", is the mildest. Look for it in tubs or plastic pouches in the produce section or Asian aisle of the supermarket.

1. Combine bonito flakes and chicken broth in medium saucepan. Bring to a boil. Strain out bonito, reserving broth.

2. Heat oil in medium saucepan. Add leek and cook over medium heat 2 to 3 minutes or until tender, stirring frequently. Add reserved broth to saucepan. Add miso; stir well. Add tofu and heat through over low heat.

Makes 4 (1 cup) servings

Beer Batter Tempura

1½ cups all-purpose flour
1½ cups Japanese beer, chilled
1 teaspoon salt
Dipping Sauce (recipe follows)
Vegetable oil for frying
½ pound green beans or asparagus tips
1 large sweet potato, peeled and cut into ¼-inch slices
1 medium eggplant, cut into ¼-inch slices

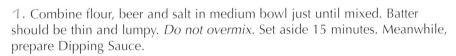

1. Combine flour, beer and salt in medium bowl just until mixed. Batter should be thin and lumpy. *Do not overmix.* Set aside 15 minutes. Meanwhile, prepare Dipping Sauce.

2. Heat 1 inch of oil in large saucepan until it reaches 375°F; adjust heat to maintain temperature.

3. Dip 10 to 12 green beans in batter; add to hot oil. Fry until light golden brown. Remove to wire racks or paper towels to drain; keep warm. Repeat with remaining vegetables, working with only one at a time and being careful not to crowd vegetables. Serve with Dipping Sauce.   *Make 4 servings*

Dipping Sauce

½ cup soy sauce
2 tablespoons rice wine
1 tablespoon sugar
½ teaspoon white vinegar
2 teaspoons minced fresh ginger
1 clove garlic, minced
2 green onions, thinly sliced

Combine soy sauce, rice wine, sugar and vinegar in small saucepan over medium heat. Cook and stir 3 minutes or until sugar dissolves. Add ginger and garlic; cook 2 minutes. Add green onions; remove from heat.

Make 4 servings

Japanese Noodle Soup

1 package (8½ ounces) Japanese udon noodles
1 teaspoon vegetable oil
1 medium red bell pepper, cut into thin strips
1 medium carrot, diagonally sliced
2 green onions, thinly sliced
2 cans (about 14 ounces each) reduced-sodium beef broth
1 cup water
1 teaspoon soy sauce
½ teaspoon grated fresh ginger
½ teaspoon black pepper
2 cups thinly sliced shiitake mushrooms, stems discarded
4 ounces daikon (Japanese radish), peeled and cut into thin strips
4 ounces firm tofu, drained and cut into ½-inch cubes

1. Cook noodles according to package directions; drain. Rinse; set aside.

2. Heat oil in large nonstick saucepan over medium-high heat. Add red bell pepper, carrot and green onions; cook about 3 minutes or until slightly softened. Stir in beef broth, water, soy sauce, ginger and black pepper; bring to a boil. Add mushrooms, daikon and tofu; reduce heat and simmer 5 minutes.

3. Place noodles in serving dishes; ladle soup over noodles.

Makes 6 servings

Chicken Gyoza

4 ounces ground chicken
¼ cup finely chopped napa cabbage
1 green onion, minced
1½ teaspoons soy sauce
½ teaspoon minced fresh ginger
½ teaspoon cornstarch
22 gyoza or wonton wrappers (about half a 10-ounce package)
2 tablespoons vegetable oil
Gyoza Dipping Sauce (recipe follows)

1. Combine chicken, cabbage, green onion, soy sauce and ginger in medium bowl. Add cornstarch and stir well.

2. Place 1 rounded teaspoonful chicken filling in center of gyoza wrapper. Dampen edges of wrapper with wet finger. Pull sides of wrapper together; press to seal semicircle. Pleat edges of gyoza by making small folds. Place on lightly oiled surface while filling remaining gyoza.

3. Heat vegetable oil in large skillet over medium heat. Add 8 to 10 gyoza to skillet; do not crowd. Cook 3 minutes per side until golden brown and filling is cooked through. Keep warm while frying remaining gyoza. Serve with Gyoza Dipping Sauce.

Makes 22 gyoza (4 to 6 appetizer servings)

Gyoza Dipping Sauce: Combine ¼ cup soy sauce, 2 teaspoons mirin (Japanese sweet rice wine) and ¼ to ½ teaspoon chili oil in small bowl. Stir well.

Chicken Gyoza

Portobello Mushrooms Sesame

2 tablespoons mirin (Japanese sweet rice wine)

2 tablespoons soy sauce

2 cloves garlic, minced

1 teaspoon dark sesame oil

4 large portobello mushroom caps

1. Prepare grill for direct cooking. Combine mirin, soy sauce, garlic and oil in small bowl.

2. Brush both sides of mushroom caps with soy sauce mixture. Grill mushrooms, top sides up, on covered grill over medium coals 3 to 4 minutes. Brush tops with soy sauce mixture; turn over. Grill 2 minutes more or until mushrooms are lightly browned. Turn again; grill, basting frequently, 4 to 5 minutes or until tender. Cut into ½-inch-thick slices.

Makes 4 servings

Japanese Pear Salad

2 tablespoons rice vinegar, red wine vinegar or balsamic vinegar

2 tablespoons packed brown sugar

2 fresh USA Anjou or Bosc pears, cored and sliced

⅓ cup thinly sliced mushrooms

¼ cup *each* thinly sliced green bell pepper and radishes

4 Green Onion Brushes (recipe follows)

Combine vinegar and sugar; gently toss pears in mixture. Allow to stand 30 minutes to 1 hour to blend flavors; stir occasionally. Drain pears and arrange with vegetables on individual plates. Garnish with Green Onion Brushes.

Makes 4 servings

Green Onion Brushes: Cut 3-inch pieces off root ends of 4 green onions. Cut three 1-inch lengthwise slashes through root end; rotate onion one half-turn and make three more 1-inch lengthwise slashes. Place in iced water. Drain before using.

*Favorite recipe from **Pear Bureau Northwest***

Grilled Bok Choy Packets

12 fresh or dried shiitake mushrooms*
½ small onion, thinly sliced
1 head bok choy (about 1 pound), coarsely chopped
1 can (about 8¾ ounces) whole baby corn, rinsed and drained
1 large red bell pepper, cut into strips
2 tablespoons water
2 tablespoons mirin (Japanese sweet rice wine)
2 tablespoons soy sauce
1½ teaspoons dark sesame oil
1 teaspoon minced fresh ginger

For dried mushrooms, place in small bowl; cover with warm water and soak 30 minutes to soften. Drain and squeeze dry.

1. Prepare grill for direct cooking. Remove and discard mushroom stems; slice caps.

2. Spray 6 (16-inch-long) sheets of foil with nonstick cooking spray. Layer onion slices, bok choy, corn, bell pepper and mushrooms in center of each sheet.

3. Combine water, mirin, soy sauce, oil and ginger in small bowl. Drizzle over vegetables in each packet.

4. Seal packets by bringing two long sides of foil together over vegetables; fold down in series of locked folds, allowing for heat circulation and expansion. Fold short ends up and over again. Press folds firmly to seal packets. Turn packets over several times to coat vegetables completely.

5. Grill packets on covered grill over medium to low coals about 10 minutes, turning every 2 to 3 minutes. (Vegetables will continue to cook once removed from heat.) To serve, carefully open one end of each packet and slide vegetables onto plates.   *Makes 6 servings*

Serving Suggestion: Grilled bok choy is great with grilled shrimp.

Japanese Yakitori

1 pound boneless skinless chicken breasts, cut into ¾-inch-wide strips
2 tablespoons sherry or pineapple juice
2 tablespoons soy sauce
1 tablespoon sugar
1 tablespoon peanut oil
½ teaspoon minced garlic
½ teaspoon minced fresh ginger
5 ounces pearl onions
½ fresh pineapple, cut into 1-inch wedges

1. Place chicken in large resealable food storage bag. Combine sherry, soy sauce, sugar, oil, garlic and ginger in small bowl; mix thoroughly to dissolve sugar. Pour into plastic bag with chicken; seal bag and turn to coat thoroughly. Refrigerate 30 minutes or up to 2 hours, turning occasionally. (If using wooden skewers, soak skewers in water 30 minutes to prevent burning.)

2. Prepare grill for direct cooking. Meanwhile, bring water to a boil in medium saucepan. Add onions; cook 4 minutes. Drain; rinse with cold water to stop cooking. Cut off root ends and slip off outer skins; set aside.

3. Drain chicken, reserving marinade. Weave chicken accordion-style onto skewers, alternating onions and pineapple with chicken. Brush with reserved marinade; discard remaining marinade.

4. Grill on uncovered grill over medium-hot coals 6 to 8 minutes or until chicken is cooked through, turning once.　　*Makes 6 servings*

Menu Classics

Tonkatsu
(Breaded Pork Cutlets)

Tonkatsu Sauce (page 218)
1 pound pork tenderloin, trimmed of fat
$\frac{1}{2}$ cup all-purpose flour
2 eggs, beaten with 2 tablespoons water
1$\frac{1}{2}$ cups panko bread crumbs
6 to 8 tablespoons vegetable oil, divided
Salt and black pepper
Hot cooked rice

1. Prepare Tonkatsu Sauce and set aside.

2. Slice pork diagonally into $\frac{1}{2}$-inch-thick pieces. Spread flour on plate and place eggs in shallow bowl. Spread panko on plate. Dip each pork slice first in flour, then egg. Shake off excess and coat in panko.

3. Heat 2 tablespoons oil in large nonstick skillet over medium heat. Add as many pork cutlets as comfortably fit; do not crowd pan. Cook over medium heat 4 minutes per side or until cooked thorough. Remove pork and drain on paper towels; keep warm. Add more oil as necessary and repeat with remaining pork.

4. Serve over rice with Tonkatsu sauce.

Makes 4 servings

continued on page 218

Tonkatsu (Breaded Pork Cutlets), continued

Tonkatsu Sauce

- ¼ **cup ketchup**
- 1 **tablespoon soy sauce**
- 2 **teaspoons sugar**
- 2 **teaspoons mirin (Japanese sweet rice wine)**
- 1 **teaspoon Worcestershire sauce**
- ½ **teaspoon grated fresh ginger**
- 1 **clove garlic, minced**

Combine ketchup, soy sauce, sugar, mirin, Worcestershire, ginger and garlic in small bowl.

Makes about ⅓ cup sauce

Teriyaki Chicken Kabobs

- ¾ **cup teriyaki sauce, divided**
- ¼ **cup pineapple juice**
- 1 **teaspoon minced garlic**
- 1 **pound boneless skinless chicken breasts, cut in 1-inch cubes**
- 2 **medium zucchini, cut in ½-inch slices**
- 1 **medium green bell pepper, cut in 1-inch squares**
- 1 **teaspoon coarse ground black pepper**
- 1 **small red onion, cut in ½-inch chunks**

1. Combine teriyaki sauce, pineapple juice and garlic. Place chicken in large resealable food storage bag; add ¾ cup teriyaki mixture. Marinate in refrigerator 30 minutes. Reserve remaining marinade.

2. Spray grid with nonstick cooking spray. Prepare grill for direct cooking. (If using wooden skewers, soak in water 30 minutes.)

3. Remove chicken from bag; discard used marinade. Alternately thread chicken, zucchini, bell pepper and onion on skewers. Sprinkle pepper on each skewer. Place on grid; grill 10 to 15 minutes until done, turning and brushing with reserved marinade.

Makes 4 to 6 servings

Teriyaki Chicken Kabobs

Miso Salmon & Spinach

1 cup sake
¼ cup white miso*
¼ cup mirin (Japanese sweet rice wine)
4 boneless skinless salmon fillets or steaks (about 5 ounces each)
1 bag (10 ounces) baby spinach
  Soy sauce
2 teaspoons sesame seeds, toasted
2 tablespoons chopped green onion (optional)

A fermented soybean paste used frequently in Japanese cooking. Miso comes in many varieties; the light yellow miso, usually labeled "white" is the mildest. Look for it in tubs or plastic pouches in the produce section or Asian aisle of the supermarket.

1. Combine sake, miso and mirin in large deep skillet or Dutch oven. Bring to a boil over high heat. Reduce heat to medium; add salmon. Simmer, uncovered, 4 minutes. Turn salmon over; simmer 3 to 4 minutes more or until salmon is opaque in center. Transfer salmon to plate and keep warm.

2. Add spinach in two batches to liquid in skillet; cook 2 minutes or until spinach is wilted. Remove spinach with slotted spoon and keep warm.

3. Turn heat to high and bring liquid to a gentle boil. Cook 1 to 2 minutes or until sauce is reduced to about ¼ cup. Season with soy sauce.

4. Serve salmon over spinach; drizzle with sauce and sprinkle with sesame seeds and green onion, if desired.   *Makes 4 servings*

Chicken Teriyaki

8 large chicken drumsticks (about 2 pounds)
$\frac{1}{3}$ cup teriyaki sauce
2 tablespoons brandy or apple juice
1 green onion, minced
1 tablespoon vegetable oil
1 teaspoon ground ginger
$\frac{1}{2}$ teaspoon sugar
$\frac{1}{4}$ teaspoon garlic powder
   Prepared sweet and sour sauce (optional)

1. Remove skin from drumsticks, if desired, by pulling skin toward end of leg using paper towel; discard skin.

2. Place chicken in large resealable food storage bag. Combine teriyaki sauce, brandy, green onion, oil, ginger, sugar and garlic powder in small bowl; pour over chicken. Close bag securely, turning to coat. Marinate in refrigerator at least 1 hour or overnight, turning occasionally.

3. Prepare grill for indirect cooking.

4. Drain chicken; reserve marinade. Place chicken on grid directly over drip pan. Grill, covered, over medium-high heat 60 minutes or until chicken is cooked through (170°F), turning and brushing with reserved marinade every 20 minutes. *Do not brush with marinade during last 5 minutes of grilling.* Discard remaining marinade. Serve with sweet and sour sauce, if desired.

Makes 4 servings

Pressed Sushi (Oshizushi)

1½ cups Japanese short grain sushi rice
3 tablespoons seasoned rice vinegar
1 large red bell pepper
1 large yellow bell pepper
1 tablespoon tamari or soy sauce
1 tablespoon mirin (Japanese sweet rice wine)
¼ cup finely chopped unpeeled cucumber
4 ounces thinly sliced smoked salmon
Salmon roe (caviar) and pickled ginger (optional)

1. Prepare rice according to package directions. Spread warm rice in large wooden bowl or on parchment lined baking sheet. Sprinkle with vinegar and gently fold vinegar into rice with wooden spoon or spatula. Cover with damp clean cloth and set aside. Do not refrigerate.

2. Meanwhile, preheat broiler. Cut bell peppers lengthwise into quarters; place skin sides up on foil lined baking sheet. Broil 3 to 4 inches from heat source 10 minutes or until skins are blackened. Wrap peppers in foil; let stand 10 minutes. Peel off and discard skins.

3. Line 8-inch square glass dish or baking pan with foil, allowing foil to extend over edges of pan for easy removal. Spoon half of rice into prepared pan; press down firmly. Arrange pepper pieces over rice in single layer covering rice completely. Combine tamari and mirin in small cup; drizzle over peppers.

4. Combine remaining rice and cucumber. Spoon evenly over peppers and press down firmly. Arrange salmon over rice covering entire surface; press down firmly. Cover salmon with plastic wrap. Place another 8-inch square baking pan on top of plastic; weight down with 2 or 3 cans of food. Let stand at room temperature 1 hour or refrigerate up to 6 hours.

5. Remove weighted pan and plastic wrap. Use foil to transfer pressed sushi to cutting board. Cut into squares or rectangles. Garnish with salmon roe and pickled ginger. *Makes 4 main dish or 8 side dish servings*

Okonomiyaki (Savory Pancake)

2 eggs
1 cup all-purpose flour
½ teaspoon salt
1 cup finely chopped cabbage
2 green onions, chopped
¾ to 1 cup water
4 teaspoons vegetable oil
   Assorted fillings:* cooked chicken or beef, red bell pepper, asparagus, corn or mushrooms

Sauce
   ¼ cup ketchup
   2 tablespoons sake
1½ tablespoons Worcestershire sauce
   1 teaspoon tamari
   ¼ teaspoon Dijon mustard

* Choose whatever fillings you like and have on hand. Okonomiyaki is a favorite Japanese snack food, enjoyed like pizza in bars and quick serve restaurants.

1. Whisk eggs, flour and salt together in medium bowl until combined. Stir in cabbage and ¾ cup water. Add enough additional water to make batter the consistency of thick pancake batter.

2. Heat a large nonstick skillet over medium-high heat. Prepare fillings. (You will need about ⅓ cup of mixed fillings for each pancake.) Brush skillet with oil. Ladle in one fourth of batter; spread into circle. Cook 2 minutes; arrange fillings on top and press gently into batter with spatula. Cook 2 to 3 minutes until edges of pancake look dull and underside is lightly browned. Turn pancake and continue cooking 2 to 4 minutes or until cooked through. Keep warm; repeat with remaining batter.

3. Meanwhile, prepare okonomiyaki sauce. Combine ketchup, sake, Worcestershire, tamari and mustard in small saucepan. Simmer for 1 minute, stirring constantly. Let cool to room temperature.

4. To serve, drizzle with sauce; cut into wedges.   Makes 4 servings

Okonomiyaki (Savory Pancake)

Fried Tofu with Sesame Dipping Sauce

3 tablespoons tamari or soy sauce

2 tablespoons unseasoned rice vinegar

2 teaspoons sugar

1 teaspoon sesame seeds, toasted*

1 teaspoon dark sesame oil

1/8 teaspoon red pepper flakes

1 block (about 12 ounces) extra firm tofu

2 tablespoons all-purpose flour

1 egg

3/4 cup panko bread crumbs

4 tablespoons vegetable oil, divided

To toast sesame seeds, spread seeds in large, dry skillet. Shake skillet over medium-low heat until seeds begin to pop and turn golden, about 3 minutes.

1. For dipping sauce, combine tamari, vinegar, sugar, sesame seeds, sesame oil and red pepper flakes in small bowl. Set aside.

2. Drain tofu and press between paper towels to remove excess water. Cut crosswise into 4 slices; cut each slice diagonally into triangles. Place flour in shallow plate. Beat egg in shallow bowl. Place panko in another shallow bowl.

3. Dip each piece of tofu lightly in flour on all sides, then in egg, turning to coat. Drain and roll in panko to coat lightly.

4. Heat 2 tablespoons vegetable oil in large nonstick skillet over high heat. Reduce heat to medium; add tofu in single layer. Cook 1 to 2 minutes per side or until golden brown. Repeat with any remaining tofu. Serve with dipping sauce.

Makes 4 servings

Fried Tofu with Sesame Dipping Sauce

Udon Noodles with Chicken & Spinach

3 tablespoons vegetable oil, divided

4 boneless skinless chicken thighs (about 12 ounces), cut into bite-size pieces

2 to 3 teaspoons grated fresh ginger

2 cloves garlic, minced

1 cup chicken broth

6 cups (6 ounces) coarsely chopped baby spinach

2 green onions, chopped

1 package (8 ounces) udon noodles, cooked and drained

1 tablespoon soy sauce

1. Heat 2 tablespoons oil in large nonstick skillet over medium heat. Add chicken and cook and stir 2 to 3 minutes or until cooked through. Remove and drain on paper towels.

2. Add remaining 1 tablespoon oil to skillet. Add ginger and garlic; cook over low heat 20 seconds or until garlic begins to color. Add chicken broth; bring to a simmer.

3. Stir in spinach and green onions. Cook 2 minutes or until spinach wilts. Stir chicken and noodles into spinach mixture. Season with soy sauce. Serve immediately.   *Makes 4 to 6 servings*

In Japan, noodles of all kinds, including udon, soba, ramen and somen, are a favorite quick, affordable meal. Noodles are served hot or cold, in soups or in bowls and are topped with fish, vegetables, tofu, meat, seaweed and just about anything else you can imagine. Slurping noodles—the louder the better—is considered not only good manners, but a compliment to the chef.

Udon Noodles with Chicken & Spinach

Teppanyaki

Ponzu Dipping Sauce (recipe follows)
4 small frozen corn on the cob, thawed
2 to 3 tablespoons vegetable oil
2 medium zucchini or yellow squash, cut diagonally into thin slices
4 ounces shiitake mushrooms, stemmed and cut into thick slices
8 ounces beef tenderloin or top loin steak, thinly sliced crosswise
8 ounces pork tenderloin, thinly sliced crosswise
8 ounces medium raw shrimp, peeled and deveined

1. Prepare Ponzu Dipping Sauce; set aside. Heat oven to 225°F to keep food warm while cooking.

2. Cook corn in microwave according to package directions just until heated through. Heat large cast iron or other heavy skillet over medium-high heat. Brush with oil. Brown corn about 2 minutes, turning frequently. Transfer to large baking pan in oven to keep warm.

3. Cook zucchini, adding oil if needed, 2 to 3 minutes or until browned and tender. Transfer to oven to keep warm. Cook mushrooms 2 to 3 minutes or until tender; keep warm.

4. Cook beef slices, adding more oil as needed, 2 minutes or until browned and tender; keep warm. Cook pork about 3 minutes; keep warm. Cook shrimp, stirring occasionally, 2 to 3 minutes or until pink and opaque.

5. Arrange vegetables and meat on warm serving plates. Serve with Ponzu Dipping Sauce. *Makes 4 servings*

Ponzu Dipping Sauce: Combine ⅓ cup tamari, 2 tablespoons mirin, 1 tablespoon lemon juice, 1 tablespoon orange juice and ⅛ teaspoon red pepper flakes in small bowl.

Serving Suggestion: Teppanyaki is often served with several dipping sauces. If you'd like to add additional dipping sauces, try the Sesame Dipping Sauce from the Fried Tofu recipe (page 228, step 1) or create a ginger dipping sauce by adding minced fresh ginger, sake and a bit of wasabi to tarmari.

Donburi (Beef & Rice Bowl)

1 cup short or medium grain white rice
3 teaspoons peanut or vegetable oil, divided
3 eggs, beaten
1 small yellow onion, cut into thin wedges
2 cups small broccoli florets
1 pound boneless beef top sirloin steak, cut crosswise into thin strips
2 teaspoons cornstarch
¼ cup beef or chicken broth
3 tablespoons tamari or soy sauce
2 teaspoons dark sesame oil
¼ teaspoon red pepper flakes
¼ cup chopped cilantro
¼ cup chopped green onions

1. Cook rice according to package directions. Meanwhile, heat 1 teaspoon peanut oil in medium skillet over medium heat. Add eggs; cook 2 minutes or until bottom of omelet is set. Turn omelet over and cook 1 minute. Slide onto cutting board; let cool. Roll up omelet and cut crosswise into thin slices; set aside.

2. Heat 1 teaspoon peanut oil in same skillet; add onion and broccoli. Cook 4 to 5 minutes, stirring occasionally; transfer to bowl. Combine beef strips and cornstarch. Heat remaining 1 teaspoon peanut oil in same skillet; stir-fry beef 2 minutes. Add broth, tamari, sesame oil and red pepper flakes. Simmer 2 minutes or until sauce thickens.

3. Stir in sliced omelet, reserved vegetables, cilantro and green onions. Stir-fry 1 minute or until heated through. Spoon rice into 4 shallow bowls; top with beef mixture.   *Makes 4 servings*

From Land & Sea

Teriyaki Salmon with Asian Slaw

4 tablespoons teriyaki sauce, divided
2 (5- to 6-ounce) salmon fillets with skin (1 inch thick)
2½ cups coleslaw mix
1 cup snow peas, cut into thin strips
½ cup thinly sliced radishes
2 tablespoons orange marmalade
1 teaspoon dark sesame oil

1. Preheat broiler or prepare grill for direct cooking. Spoon 2 tablespoons teriyaki sauce over fleshy sides of salmon. Let stand while preparing vegetable mixture.

2. Combine coleslaw mix, snow peas and radishes in large bowl. Combine remaining 2 tablespoons teriyaki sauce, marmalade and sesame oil in small bowl. Add to coleslaw mixture; toss well.

3. Broil salmon 4 to 5 inches from heat source or grill, flesh side down, over medium coals, without turning, 6 to 10 minutes or until center is opaque.

4. Transfer coleslaw mixture to serving plates; serve with salmon.

Makes 2 servings

Japanese Fried Chicken on Watercress

1 pound boneless skinless chicken breasts, cut into 2-inch pieces
3 tablespoons tamari or soy sauce
2 tablespoons sake
3 cloves garlic, minced
1 teaspoon minced fresh ginger
   Oil for deep frying
$\frac{1}{3}$ cup cornstarch
3 tablespoons all-purpose flour

Salad

$\frac{1}{4}$ cup unseasoned rice vinegar
3 teaspoons tamari or soy sauce
1 teaspoon dark sesame oil
2 bunches watercress, trimmed of tough stems and coarsely chopped
1 pint grape tomatoes, halved

1. Place chicken in resealable food storage bag. Mix 3 tablespoons tamari, sake, garlic and ginger in small bowl. Pour over chicken and marinate in refrigerator at least 30 minutes, turning bag occasionally.

2. Meanwhile, heat at least 1½ inches oil to 350°F in deep heavy saucepan over medium high. Combine cornstarch and flour in shallow dish. Drain chicken and discard marinade. Roll chicken pieces in cornstarch mixture and shake off excess.

3. Deep fry chicken in batches 4 to 6 minutes or until golden and cooked through. Do not crowd pan. Drain on paper towels.

4. For salad dressing, whisk together vinegar, 3 teaspoons tamari and sesame oil in small bowl. Arrange watercress and tomatoes on serving plates, drizzle with dressing and top with chicken.   *Makes 4 servings*

California Roll Sushi

Sushi Rice (recipe page 242)
3 sheets toasted nori (from .6 ounce package)
9 tablespoons crabmeat
6 baby carrots, cut into matchstick-size pieces
1 avocado, peeled, pitted and cut into thin lengthwise slices
Soy sauce, prepared wasabi and pickled ginger

1. Prepare Sushi Rice and reserve, covered, at room temperature. Prepare small bowl with water and splash of rice vinegar to rinse fingers and prevent rice from sticking to hands while working. Place sheet of nori, shiny side down, on bamboo rolling mat (lined with plastic wrap, if desired) with wide side of nori aligned with edge closest to you.

2. Wet fingers and spread about 1 cup rice over nori. Leave $\frac{1}{2}$-inch border at top edge of nori to seal roll.

3. Arrange 3 tablespoons crabmeat crosswise on rice about $1\frac{1}{2}$ inches from bottom of nori. Add carrot pieces over crabmeat. Place 2 or 3 avocado slices next to carrots.

4. Working from bottom, firmly roll up nori sheet into 8-inch log. Press gently to compact rice and keep fillings centered. When roll is completed, press gently to seal and place seam side down on cutting board.

5. Repeat with remaining nori and fillings. Cut each roll into 6 pieces using sharp knife; wipe knife with wet cloth between cuts to slice cleanly. Serve with soy sauce and wasabi for dipping and pickled ginger.

Makes 6 (3-piece) servings

continued on page 242

California Roll Sushi, continued

Sushi Rice

1 cup Japanese short grain sushi rice*
1¼ cups water (plus water for rinsing)
2 tablespoons unseasoned rice vinegar**
4 teaspoons sugar
½ teaspoon salt

*If you can't find white rice labeled "sushi rice", use any short grain white rice.

**Or use seasoned rice vinegar and skip adding salt and sugar.

1. Place rice in strainer with small holes. Rinse in cold water until water runs clear. Drain thoroughly. Place rice in saucepan with 1¼ cups water. Bring to a boil; stir. Reduce heat to very low, cover saucepan and cook for 20 minutes or until water is absorbed. Do not lift lid while cooking. Remove from heat; let sit 5 minutes.

2. Combine rice vinegar, sugar and salt in small microwavable bowl or measuring cup. Microwave on HIGH 30 seconds and stir to dissolve sugar.

3. Using wooden spoon transfer rice to shallow wooden or glass bowl. Sprinkle on vinegar mixture; fold into rice gently, taking care not to crush or break rice grains. *Makes 3 cups*

The rice itself is one of the most important elements in making sushi. It is rinsed to remove some starch and make it a little less sticky and cooked with a bit less water than usual since it will absorb moisture from the vinegar dressing. Traditionally the cooked rice is spread out in a special shallow wooden tub, called a "hangiri," to cool. It is fanned while the vinegar is gently mixed in, to create a good texture and gloss. The aim is to cool the rice quickly without breaking too many grains.

Roast Sesame Fish

4 tilapia fillets (about 5 ounces each)
1/4 cup plus 1 tablespoon tamari or soy sauce, divided
1 teaspoon dark sesame oil, divided
2 teaspoons sesame seeds
2 tablespoons sake
1 teaspoon wasabi paste
1 teaspoon sugar
2 to 3 teaspoons grated fresh ginger

1. Preheat oven to 400°F. Place fish in shallow baking dish. Combine 1 tablespoon tamari and 1/2 teaspoon sesame oil; brush over fish. Sprinkle sesame seeds over fish. Bake 10 to 15 minutes or until fish is opaque in center.

2. Meanwhile, combine remaining 1/4 cup tamari, 1/2 teaspoon sesame oil, sake, wasabi paste, sugar and ginger in small bowl. Drizzle sauce over fish before serving. *Makes 4 servings*

Ginger is the root (more accurately, a rhizome) of a tropical plant and is used in a variety of different forms in Asian cooking. The fresh root should have smooth skin and a fresh, spicy fragrance. Pickled ginger, which is used in this recipe, is thinly sliced ginger preserved in a sweet vinegar and sold in jars. It is most often seen as a garnish with sushi. Store pickled ginger in its original container in your refrigerator.

Wasabi Salmon

2 tablespoons soy sauce
1½ teaspoons prepared wasabi
4 salmon fillets with skin (6 ounces each)
¼ cup mayonnaise

1. Prepare grill for direct cooking or preheat broiler.

2. Combine soy sauce and ½ teaspoon wasabi; mix well. Spoon mixture over salmon.

3. Place salmon, skin sides down, on grid over medium coals or on rack of broiler pan. Grill or broil 4 to 5 inches from heat 8 minutes or until salmon is opaque in center.

4. Meanwhile, combine mayonnaise and remaining 1 teaspoon wasabi paste; mix well. Taste and add more wasabi, if desired. Transfer salmon to serving plates; top with wasabi mixture.   *Makes 4 servings*

Wasabi is sometimes referred to as Japanese horseradish. It has a fiery flavor and is the green paste usually served with sushi. Wasabi is available in a powdered form, which must be mixed with water to form a paste, or in a squeezable tube, which is ready to use. You'll find wasabi powder in the Asian section of most large supermarkets.

Teriyaki Scallops

2 tablespoons soy sauce
1 tablespoon mirin (Japanese sweet rice wine)
2 teaspoons sake or dry sherry
1 teaspoon sugar
1 pound large scallops
¼ teaspoon salt
8 ounces asparagus, diagonally sliced into 2-inch lengths
1 tablespoon vegetable oil

1. Combine soy sauce, mirin, sake and sugar in medium bowl; stir until sugar is dissolved. Add scallops; let stand 10 minutes, turning occasionally.

2. Meanwhile, bring 2½ cups water and salt to a boil in medium saucepan over high heat. Add asparagus; reduce heat to medium-high. Cook 3 to 5 minutes or until crisp-tender. Drain asparagus; keep warm.

3. Drain scallops, reserving marinade.

4. Preheat broiler. Line broiler pan with foil; brush broiler rack with vegetable oil. Place scallops on rack; brush lightly with marinade. Broil about 4 inches from heat source 4 to 5 minutes or until brown. Turn scallops with tongs; brush lightly with marinade. Broil 4 to 5 minutes or just until scallops are opaque in center. Serve immediately with asparagus.

Makes 4 servings

Stuffed Vegetable Tempura

½ **cup all-purpose flour**

2 **tablespoons plus** ½ **teaspoon cornstarch, divided**

1 **teaspoon baking powder**

¼ **teaspoon salt**

¾ **cup cold water**

1 **egg, separated**

1 **pound large raw shrimp, peeled and deveined**

1 **tablespoon soy sauce**

2 **teaspoons dark sesame oil**

Soy Dipping Sauce (recipe page 250)

4 **cups vegetable oil**

1 **zucchini, diagonally cut into** ½-**inch-thick slices**

8 **button mushrooms, stems removed**

1 **red bell pepper, cut into wedges**

1 **green bell pepper, cut into wedges**

Lemon wedges (optional)

1. Place flour, 2 tablespoons cornstarch, baking powder and salt in medium bowl; mix well with wire whisk. Make well in center and whisk in water until batter is consistency of pancake batter with small lumps. Add egg white to batter; whisk until blended. Cover and refrigerate 30 minutes.

2. Meanwhile, place egg yolk in food processor. Add shrimp, soy sauce, sesame oil and remaining ½ teaspoon cornstarch to food processor. Process until shrimp is chopped to a paste. Place shrimp paste in small bowl; cover and refrigerate.

3. Prepare Soy Dipping Sauce and keep warm.

4. Heat vegetable oil in wok or deep heavy saucepan over medium-high heat until oil registers 375°F on deep-fry thermometer. Spread about 1½ to 2 teaspoons shrimp paste on 8 zucchini slices and stuff remaining paste into mushroom caps and pepper wedges.

continued on page 250

Stuffed Vegetable Tempura, continued

5. Stir batter and dip stuffed vegetables into batter. Carefully add to oil in batches, stuffing side up. Fry about 2 minutes for peppers, 3 minutes for zucchini and 4 minutes for mushrooms or until golden brown, turning once. Drain on paper towels. Dip leftover zucchini slices into remaining batter and fry about 3 minutes or until golden brown.

7. To serve, arrange vegetables on plates. Serve with Soy Dipping Sauce and lemon wedges, if desired.   Makes 4 servings

Soy Dipping Sauce

1 cup reduced-sodium chicken broth
3 tablespoons soy sauce
2 tablespoons sugar
1 tablespoon sake or rice wine
½ teaspoon minced fresh ginger

Place all ingredients in small saucepan; bring to a boil over low heat.

Makes about 1¼ cups

Tuna Teriyaki

4 fresh tuna steaks (about 1½ pounds)
¼ cup soy sauce
2 tablespoons sake
1 tablespoon sugar
½ teaspoon minced fresh ginger
¼ teaspoon minced garlic
1½ tablespoons vegetable oil
2 small limes, cut into halves
Pickled ginger (optional)

*Substitute salmon, halibut, swordfish or other firm-fleshed fish, if desired.

1. Cut tuna into 4 equal pieces; place in single layer in shallow bowl.

2. Combine soy sauce, sake, sugar, minced ginger and garlic in small bowl; stir until sugar is dissolved.

3. Pour soy marinade over tuna. Marinate in refrigerator, turning frequently, 40 minutes.

4. Drain tuna, reserving marinade. Heat oil in large skillet over medium heat. Add tuna; cook until light brown, 2 to 3 minutes. Turn tuna over; cook just until opaque, 2 to 3 minutes.

5. Reduce heat to medium-low; pour reserved marinade over tuna. Add limes to skillet, cut side down. Cook, turning tuna once, until coated and sauce is bubbly, 1 to 1½ minutes.

6. Serve immediately with limes and pickled ginger.

Makes 4 servings

Grilled Swordfish with Hot Red Sauce

½ **cup sesame seeds**
¼ **teaspoon salt**
4 **swordfish or halibut steaks (about 1½ pounds total)**
¼ **cup finely chopped green onions**
2 **tablespoons hot bean paste***
2 **tablespoons soy sauce**
4 **teaspoons sugar**
4 **cloves garlic, minced**
1 **tablespoon dark sesame oil**
⅛ **teaspoon black pepper**

*Available in specialty stores or Asian markets.

1. Heat small skillet over medium heat. Add sesame seeds; cook and stir about 3 minutes or until seeds become fragrant. Cool; place with salt in small spice grinder. Process just until crushed.

2. Spray grid of grill or broiler rack with nonstick cooking spray. Prepare coals for direct cooking or preheat broiler.

3. Rinse swordfish and pat dry with paper towels. Place in shallow glass dish.

4. Combine green onions, crushed sesame mixture, hot bean paste, soy sauce, sugar, garlic, sesame oil and pepper in small bowl; mix well.

5. Spread half of marinade over fish; turn fish over and spread with remaining marinade. Cover with plastic wrap and refrigerate 30 minutes.

6. Remove fish from marinade; discard marinade. Place fish on prepared grid. Grill fish over medium-hot coals or broil 4 to 5 minutes per side or until fish is opaque. *Makes 4 servings*

Grilled Swordfish with Hot Red Sauce

Teriyaki Grilled Snapper

2 whole red snappers or striped bass (1½ pounds each), scaled and gutted
⅓ cup *French's*® Worcestershire Sauce
⅓ cup peanut oil
⅓ cup rice vinegar
¼ cup chopped green onion
1 tablespoon dark sesame oil
1 tablespoon chopped peeled fresh ginger
3 cloves garlic, chopped
   Asian Slaw (recipe follows)

Rinse fish and place in large resealable plastic food storage bag or shallow glass dish. To prepare marinade, place Worcestershire, peanut oil, vinegar, onion, sesame oil, ginger and garlic in food processor or blender. Cover and process until well blended. Reserve ¼ cup marinade for serving. Pour remaining marinade over fish. Seal bag or cover dish and marinate in refrigerator 1 hour.

Place fish in oiled grilling basket, reserving marinade for basting. Grill over medium-high coals 10 to 12 minutes per side or until fish flakes when tested with fork, basting occasionally with basting marinade. (Do not baste during last 5 minutes of cooking.) Discard any unused marinade. Carefully remove bones from fish. Pour reserved ¼ cup marinade over fish. Serve with Asian Slaw. Garnish as desired.   Makes 4 servings

Prep Time: 10 minutes
Marinate Time: 1 hour
Cook Time: 25 minutes

Asian Slaw

½ small head napa cabbage, shredded (about 4 cups)*
3 carrots, shredded
2 red or yellow bell peppers, seeded and cut into very thin strips
¼ pound snow peas, trimmed and cut into thin strips
⅓ cup peanut oil
¼ cup rice vinegar
3 tablespoons *French's®* Worcestershire Sauce
1 tablespoon dark sesame oil
1 tablespoon honey
2 cloves garlic, minced

You can substitute 4 cups shredded green cabbage for the napa cabbage.

Place vegetables in large bowl. Whisk together peanut oil, vinegar, Worcestershire, sesame oil, honey and garlic in small bowl until well blended. Pour dressing over vegetables; toss well to coat evenly. Cover and refrigerate 1 hour before serving. *Makes 4 to 6 servings*

Prep Time: 20 minutes
Chill Time: 1 hour

Napa cabbage is often called Chinese cabbage and, to confuse things even further, is also referred to as Peking cabbage or celery cabbage. Napa cabbage is long instead of round with heavily veined leaves that are almost white with green tips. The flavor is milder than regular cabbage and the texture is light, crisp and less waxy. Choose tightly packed heads without yellowing or cracking.

Japanese American

Teriyaki Steak with Onions and Mushrooms

1 boneless beef sirloin steak, about 1 inch thick (1½ pounds)
¾ cup light teriyaki sauce, divided
1 tablespoon vegetable oil
1 can (8 ounces) sliced mushrooms, drained
1 small red or green bell pepper, cut into strips
1⅓ cups *French's*® French Fried Onions, divided

1. Brush each side of steak with 1 tablespoon teriyaki sauce. Heat oil in grill pan or heavy skillet over medium-high heat. Cook steak for 3 to 4 minutes per side or until desired doneness. Remove steak; keep warm.

2. Add mushrooms and bell pepper to pan; cook until pepper is crisp-tender. Stir in remaining teriyaki sauce and ⅔ *cup* French Fried Onions; heat through.

3. Serve mushroom mixture over steak. Sprinkle with remaining onions.   *Makes 6 servings*

Prep Time: 5 minutes
Cook Time: 15 minutes

Asian Noodles with Vegetables and Chicken

- 1 tablespoon vegetable oil
- 2 cups sliced shiitake or button mushrooms
- 2 cups snow peas, sliced in half
- 2 packages (1.6 ounces each) garlic and vegetable instant rice noodle soup mix
- 2 cups boiling water
- 12 ounces cooked chicken, cut into pieces
- ¼ teaspoon red pepper flakes
- 2 tablespoons lime juice
- 1 tablespoon soy sauce
- 2 tablespoons chopped fresh cilantro or sliced green onion

1. Heat oil in large skillet over medium-high heat. Add mushrooms and snow peas; cook 2 to 3 minutes or until snow peas are crisp-tender. Remove from skillet; set aside.

2. Break up noodles in soup mix. Add noodles, 1 seasoning packet, water, chicken and red pepper flakes to skillet; mix well. Cook over medium-high heat 5 to 7 minutes or until liquid thickens. Stir in reserved vegetables, lime juice and soy sauce. Sprinkle with cilantro. Serve immediately.

Makes 4 servings

Beef Teriyaki Stir-Fry

1 cup uncooked rice
1 boneless beef top sirloin steak (about 1 pound)
½ cup teriyaki sauce, divided
2 tablespoons vegetable oil, divided
1 medium onion, halved and sliced
2 cups green beans

1. Cook rice according to package directions.

2. Cut beef lengthwise in half, then crosswise into ⅛-inch slices. Combine beef and ¼ cup teriyaki sauce in medium bowl; set aside.

3. Heat 1½ teaspoons oil in wok or large skillet over medium-high heat. Add onion; stir-fry 3 to 4 minutes or until crisp-tender. Remove from wok to medium bowl.

4. Heat 1½ teaspoons oil in wok. Stir-fry beans 3 minutes or until crisp-tender and hot. Drain off excess liquid. Add beans to onions in bowl.

5. Heat remaining 1 tablespoon oil in wok. Drain beef, discarding marinade. Stir-fry half of beef 2 minutes or until barely pink in center. Remove to bowl. Repeat with remaining beef. Return cooked beef and accumulated juice to wok. Stir in vegetables and remaining ¼ cup teriyaki sauce; cook and stir 1 minute or until heated through. Serve with rice.   *Makes 4 servings*

Prep and Cook Time: 22 minutes

Asian Wraps

Nonstick cooking spray

8 ounces boneless skinless chicken breasts or thighs, cut into ½-inch pieces

1 teaspoon minced fresh ginger

1 teaspoon minced garlic

¼ teaspoon red pepper flakes

¼ cup teriyaki sauce

4 cups (about 8 ounces) packaged coleslaw mix

½ cup sliced green onions

4 (10-inch) flour tortillas

8 teaspoons plum fruit spread

1. Spray nonstick wok or large skillet with cooking spray; heat over medium-high heat. Stir-fry chicken 2 minutes. Add ginger, garlic and hot pepper flakes; stir-fry 2 minutes. Add teriyaki sauce; mix well.* Add coleslaw mix and green onions; stir-fry 4 minutes or until chicken is cooked through and cabbage is crisp-tender.

2. Spread each tortilla with 2 teaspoons fruit spread; evenly spoon chicken mixture down center of tortillas. Roll up to form wraps.

Makes 4 servings

If sauce is too thick, add up to 2 tablespoons water to thin it.

Prep Time: 10 minutes
Cook Time: 10 minutes

Pineapple Teriyaki Chicken

½ **small red onion, halved and thinly sliced**
1 **medium green and/or red bell pepper, cut into 1-inch pieces**
6 **boneless, skinless chicken breasts (about 1½ pounds)**
1 **can (20 ounces) pineapple rings, drained**
1 **cup LAWRY'S® Teriyaki Marinade, divided**

Preheat oven to 375°F. Spray 13×9×2-inch glass baking dish with nonstick cooking spray; add onion and bell pepper. Arrange chicken over vegetables. Top with pineapple, then drizzle with Marinade. Bake 40 minutes, or until chicken is thoroughly cooked. Spoon pan juices over chicken and vegetables once during baking and again just before serving.   *Makes 6 servings*

Tender Beef Teriyaki Skewers

1 **can (20 ounces) DOLE® Pineapple Chunks**
1 **pound beef top round steak, cut into ¾-inch pieces**
½ **cup bottled honey teriyaki or teriyaki marinade and sauce, divided**
½ **large DOLE® Green or Red Bell Pepper, cut into chunks**
  Hot cooked rice (optional)

• Place steak in shallow non-metallic dish. Pour ¼ cup teriyaki sauce over steak. Cover; marinate 15 minutes in refrigerator.

• Thread pineapple chunks, steak and bell peppers onto skewers. Brush with remaining marinade.

• Grill or broil 8 to 12 minutes, turning and brushing occasionally with marinade during grilling. Discard any remaining marinade. Serve with rice, if desired.   *Makes 4 servings*

Pineapple Teriyaki Chicken

Easy Teriyaki Burgers

½ cup ketchup
2 tablespoons teriyaki sauce
½ teaspoon black pepper
1 pound ground beef
4 kaiser rolls or hamburger buns, warmed
4 leaves green leaf lettuce
4 slices tomato

1. Prepare grill for direct cooking.

2. Combine ketchup, teriyaki sauce and pepper in small bowl. Add ¼ cup mixture to ground beef; mix well. Shape beef into four ½-inch-thick patties.

3. Place patties on grid over medium heat. Grill, covered, 8 to 10 minutes (or, uncovered, 13 to 15 minutes) to medium doneness (160°F), turning and brushing often with remaining sauce. Place patties on buns. Serve with lettuce and tomato slices.   *Makes 4 servings*

Prep Time: 5 minutes
Cook Time: 15 minutes

Easy Teriyaki Burger

Ham and Cheese "Sushi" Rolls

4 thin slices deli ham (about 4×4 inches)
1 package (8 ounces) cream cheese, softened
1 piece (4 inches long) seedless cucumber, quartered lengthwise
4 thin slices (about 4×4 inches) American or Cheddar cheese, at room temperature
1 red bell pepper, cut into thin 4-inch-long strips

1. For ham sushi, pat 1 ham slice with paper towel to remove excess moisture. Spread 2 tablespoons cream cheese to edges of ham slice. Pat 1 cucumber piece with paper towel to remove excess moisture; place at edge of ham slice. Roll up tightly, pressing gently to seal. Wrap in plastic wrap; refrigerate. Repeat with remaining ham slices, cream cheese and cucumber pieces.

2. For cheese sushi, spread 2 tablespoons cream cheese to edges of 1 cheese slice. Place 2 red pepper strips at edge of cheese slice. Roll up tightly, pressing gently to seal. Wrap in plastic wrap; refrigerate. Repeat with remaining cheese slices, cream cheese and red pepper strips.

3. To serve, remove plastic wrap from ham and cheese rolls. Cut each roll into 8 pieces.   *Makes 64 pieces*

Orange Teriyaki Pork Packets

½ pound lean pork stew meat (1-inch cubes)
1½ cups frozen bell pepper blend for stir-fry
¼ cup water chestnuts, coarsely chopped
2 sheets (18×12 inches) heavy-duty foil, lightly sprayed with nonstick cooking spray
1 tablespoon cornstarch
2 tablespoons teriyaki sauce
2 tablespoons orange marmalade
½ teaspoon dry mustard
¼ teaspoon ground ginger
Hot cooked rice

1. Preheat oven to 450°F.

2. Combine pork, bell pepper blend and water chestnuts in medium bowl; toss to mix. Place half of mixture on each foil sheet.

3. Dissolve cornstarch in teriyaki sauce in small bowl. Stir in marmalade, mustard and ginger. Pour mixture over pork and vegetables.

4. Double fold sides and ends of foil to seal packets, leaving head space for heat circulation. Place packets on baking sheet.

5. Bake 20 to 23 minutes or until pork is tender. Remove from oven. Carefully open one end of each packet to allow steam to escape. Open packets and transfer contents to serving plates. Serve with rice.   *Makes 2 servings*

Asian Marinated Flank Steak

1 pound beef flank steak

¼ cup soy sauce

2 tablespoons rice vinegar or white wine vinegar

1 tablespoon chili garlic sauce *or* 1 teaspoon hot chili oil

2 teaspoons dark sesame oil

2 tablespoons chopped fresh cilantro (optional)

1. Place steak in resealable food storage bag. Combine soy sauce, vinegar, chili garlic sauce and sesame oil; pour over steak in bag. Close bag securely. Turn to coat steak on all sides. Refrigerate at least 2 hours or up to 48 hours.

2. Prepare grill for direct cooking or preheat broiler. Remove steak from bag; discard marinade. Grill steak over medium-hot coals on a covered grill or broil, 3 to 4 inches from heat source, 4 to 5 minutes per side for medium-rare to medium doneness (160°F). (Do not overcook or steak will be tough.) Transfer steak to carving board. Tent with foil and let stand 5 minutes. Carve steak crosswise across grain into thin slices; garnish with cilantro.

Makes 4 (3-ounce) servings

Serving suggestion: Serve with brown rice and a salad of thinly sliced cucumber and white onion splashed with rice vinegar and a pinch of sugar.

Glazed Teriyaki Chicken Stir-Fry Sub

¼ cup *French's®* Honey Dijon Mustard
2 tablespoons teriyaki sauce
1 tablespoon sucralose sugar substitute
1 tablespoon grated, peeled ginger root
1 tablespoon cider or red wine vinegar
1 tablespoon vegetable oil
1 pound boneless skinless chicken, cut into thin strips
1 cup coarsely chopped red or yellow bell peppers
½ cup *each* coarsely chopped red onion and plum tomatoes
2 cups shredded Napa cabbage or romaine lettuce
4 Italian hero rolls, split (about 8 inches each)

1. Combine mustard, teriyaki sauce, sugar substitute, ginger and vinegar in small bowl; set aside.

2. Heat oil in large skillet or wok over high heat. Stir-fry chicken 5 minutes until no longer pink. Add vegetables and stir-fry 2 minutes until just tender. Pour sauce mixture over stir-fry and cook 1 minute.

3. Arrange cabbage on rolls and top with equal portions of stir-fry. Close rolls. Serve warm.   Makes 4 servings

Low-Carb Tip: To reduce carbs to 10g net per serving, omit rolls and serve on shredded Napa cabbage.

Tip: If desired, substitute 1 pound sliced boneless pork or steak for the chicken.

Prep Time: 10 minutes
Cook Time: 8 minutes

Glazed Teriyaki Chicken
Stir-Fry Sub

Citrus Ginger Teriyaki Steak

1 boneless beef top sirloin steak, cut 1 inch thick (about 1 pound)
½ cup water

Marinade & Sauce:
   ½ cup prepared teriyaki marinade and sauce
   ⅓ cup orange marmalade
   2 tablespoons creamy peanut butter
   1 tablespoon finely chopped ginger
   3 large garlic cloves, crushed
   2 teaspoons dark sesame oil

1. Combine marinade ingredients in small saucepan over medium heat, whisking just until blended. Remove from heat. Place steak and ⅓ cup marinade mixture in plastic bag; turn steak to coat. Close bag securely and marinate in refrigerator 30 minutes, turning once. Reserve remaining marinade mixture for sauce.

2. Remove steak from marinade; discard marinade. Place steak on rack in broiler pan so surface of beef is 3 to 4 inches from heat. Broil steak 16 to 21 minutes for medium rare to medium doneness, turning once.

3. Meanwhile add water to reserved sauce in small saucepan; bring to a boil. Reduce heat and simmer 12 to 15 minutes or until slightly thickened, stirring occasionally.

4. Carve steak into slices. Serve steak with sauce.   Makes 4 servings.

Tip: To grill, place the steak on grid over medium, ash-colored coals. Grill, uncovered, 17 to 21 minutes for medium-rare to medium doneness, turning occasionally.

Prep and Cook Time: 30 minutes
Marinating Time: 30 minutes

Favorite recipe from **National Cattlemen's Beef Association on Behalf of The Beef Checkoff**

Acknowledgments

The publisher would like to thank the companies and organizations listed below for the use of their recipes and photographs in this publication.

ACH Food Companies, Inc.

Birds Eye Foods

California Tree Fruit Agreement

Delmarva Poultry Industry, Inc.

Del Monte Corporation

Dole Food Company, Inc.

Florida Department of Agriculture and Consumer Services, Bureau of Seafood and Aquaculture

Hormel Foods, LLC

Jennie-O Turkey Store, LLC

Lee Kum Kee (USA) Inc.

MASTERFOODS USA

McIlhenny Company (TABASCO® brand Pepper Sauce)

National Cattlemen's Beef Association on Behalf of The Beef Checkoff

National Fisheries Institute

National Honey Board

Pacific Northwest Canned Pear Service

Peanut Advisory Board

Pear Bureau Northwest

Reckitt Benckiser Inc.

Unilever

USA Rice Federation™

VOLUME MEASUREMENTS (dry)

1/8 teaspoon = 0.5 mL
1/4 teaspoon = 1 mL
1/2 teaspoon = 2 mL
3/4 teaspoon = 4 mL
1 teaspoon = 5 mL
1 tablespoon = 15 mL
2 tablespoons = 30 mL
1/4 cup = 60 mL
1/3 cup = 75 mL
1/2 cup = 125 mL
2/3 cup = 150 mL
3/4 cup = 175 mL
1 cup = 250 mL
2 cups = 1 pint = 500 mL
3 cups = 750 mL
4 cups = 1 quart = 1 L

VOLUME MEASUREMENTS (fluid)

1 fluid ounce (2 tablespoons) = 30 mL
4 fluid ounces (1/2 cup) = 125 mL
8 fluid ounces (1 cup) = 250 mL
12 fluid ounces (1 1/2 cups) = 375 mL
16 fluid ounces (2 cups) = 500 mL

WEIGHTS (mass)

1/2 ounce = 15 g
1 ounce = 30 g
3 ounces = 90 g
4 ounces = 120 g
8 ounces = 225 g
10 ounces = 285 g
12 ounces = 360 g
16 ounces = 1 pound = 450 g

DIMENSIONS

1/16 inch = 2 mm
1/8 inch = 3 mm
1/4 inch = 6 mm
1/2 inch = 1.5 cm
3/4 inch = 2 cm
1 inch = 2.5 cm

OVEN TEMPERATURES

250°F = 120°C
275°F = 140°C
300°F = 150°C
325°F = 160°C
350°F = 180°C
375°F = 190°C
400°F = 200°C
425°F = 220°C
450°F = 230°C

BAKING PAN SIZES

Utensil	Size in Inches/Quarts	Metric Volume	Size in Centimeters
Baking or Cake Pan (square or rectangular)	8×8×2	2 L	20×20×5
	9×9×2	2.5 L	23×23×5
	12×8×2	3 L	30×20×5
	13×9×2	3.5 L	33×23×5
Loaf Pan	8×4×3	1.5 L	20×10×7
	9×5×3	2 L	23×13×7
Round Layer Cake Pan	8×1½	1.2 L	20×4
	9×1½	1.5 L	23×4
Pie Plate	8×1¼	750 mL	20×3
	9×1¼	1 L	23×3
Baking Dish or Casserole	1 quart	1 L	—
	1½ quart	1.5 L	—
	2 quart	2 L	—